WOMEN
IN TUNE

Other books by the author:

My Glimpse of Eternity

Prayers That Are Answered

Super Natural Living

Angels Watching Over Me

WOMEN IN TUNE

Betty Malz

Published by
√ chosen books

FLEMING H. REVELL COMPANY
OLD TAPPAN, NEW JERSEY

Unless otherwise noted, Scripture is taken from the King James Version of the Bible. NIV: The Holy Bible, New International Version, © 1978 by the International Bible Society, used by permission of Zondervan Bible Publishers.

Library of Congress Cataloging-in-Publication Data

Malz, Betty.
Women in tune.
"A Chosen book"—T.p. verso.
1. Women—Religious life.   2. Malz, Betty.
I.   Title.
BV4527.M25   1987   248.8'43   87-23384
ISBN 0–8007–9112–6

A Chosen Book
Copyright © 1987 by Betty Malz
Chosen Books are published by
Fleming H. Revell Company
Old Tappan, New Jersey
Printed in the United States of America

This book is dedicated to my girls . . .

A, B, C, C, and D:

April, my daughter, in tune with health, sports, and humor. She is a senior at Wheaton College.

Brenda, my daughter, in tune with music and people. She teaches music, writes, and is very sensitive to the needs of others. She lives in North Carolina with her husband and two children.

Connie, my stepdaughter, in tune with children and change. She has adjusted well to life's changes. She and her children live in North Dakota.

Carol, my stepdaughter, in tune with nature and outdoors. She lives in Vail, Colorado, with her husband and son.

Diane, our only daughter-in-law, married to Carl David. She is in tune with men and good music. She is a fine wife and the mother of sons. They live in Mooresville, North Carolina.

ACKNOWLEDGMENTS

Thanks to Evelyn Bence for her editorial expertise and finishing touch.

To Jane Campbell and Ann McMath for the initial challenge and suggestion that I do a book of this nature.

To my husband, Carl, private coach and daily prayer partner. He loves feminine tenderness, but taught me to persist, exercised brutal honesty, and spurred me on.

To Mavis Jundt, my neighbor and unknowing stabilizer as I came and went.

To Sandy Anderson. I anonymously studied her personality.

I appreciate the following "In Tune" friends for suggestions, stories and contributions:

Dawn Wagler	Pat Kemp
Marilyn Kingsriter	Mary Pallesen
Karla Norton	Esther Zink
Joyce Simmons	Hannah Hyde
Madge Stack	Ona Heuser
Sandra LeSourd	Dayton Kingsriter

Jeanne and Charlie Cundiff
Tracy and Paul Hamelink
Julie and Jim Talerico

CONTENTS

9

INTRODUCTION

Don't ask the pastor on Sunday if a woman is in tune.

Ask her son on Monday morning when the school bus is honking, the phone ringing, the dog barking, and the bacon burning.

Ask her hairdresser on Tuesday after a bad perm.

Ask her doctor on Wednesday when he tells her she is pregnant again.

Ask her neighbor on Thursday in the alley.

Ask her boss on Friday.

Ask her husband on Saturday night.

Any woman can develop a specialty, put on a performance. But what about the day-in, day-out living patterns that make life steady and joyful?

When you are out of tune with God, you lose your peace and eventually your soul.

When you are out of tune with others, you lose your identity.

When you are out of tune with other women, you lose understanding, friendship, and support.

When you are out of tune with your one special man, you lose your security.

When you are out of tune with yourself, you lose your motivation.

When you are out of tune with change, you lose a sense of reality.

When you are out of tune with aging, you lose control.

When you are out of tune with nature, you lose your health.

When you are out of tune with humor, you lose your joy.

When you are out of tune with simplicity, you lose life's answers.

Satan recognized woman's power of influence, so he devised to short-circuit God's plan by appealing to the first woman, Eve. Her imagination sidetracked her out of synchronization with God, and out of tune with her husband. Many flawed females still self-destruct when they "think" with their glands.

God knew the powerful influence of woman. He mastered a plan, introduced hope to humanity, and redeemed the world through the womb of a healthy, sensitive, cooperative, "in tune" woman, Mary.

I believe that God has secrets and treasures that He wants to reveal to women today who will tune in to Him with simple, uncomplicated faith.

Are women more spiritual than men?

Statistics seem to indicate that women do "tune in" spiritually more than men. Eighty percent of religious and inspirational books are purchased by women. Ninety percent of the couples who attend my husband's marriage seminars are there because the woman took the initiative. Sixty percent of church members are female.

Dr. Paul Yonggi Cho's church in Seoul, Korea, has more than 500,000 members. The growth explosion is basically a direct result of prayer cell groups, primarily made up of women.

Oswald J. Smith kept a daily diary of the great revival moves around the world. He found out they started with "aware," in-tune-with-God women who were sensitive to reality and need.

When my editors asked me to write a book that could help women stay in tune, I was excited. I envisioned a practical guidebook, speaking frankly to women's need for "fine-tuning" the most pressing aspects of their lives. I have conducted women's retreats in forty-six states. I often lead a session called "You Asked for It!" We pass out 3x5 cards and ask each woman to write down three things: her deepest personal need, an unanswered question about life, and a prayer request. In this book I have addressed the priority needs from these seminars.

I have never professed being good at this sort of thing. I write as I speak, cafeteria-style. I deliver a few telegrams and pass out a few prescriptions. Mostly I just listen and take dictation. I don't have all the answers, but I have a Friend who is everywhere, can do anything, and has promised to give me the answers if I but ask. The Bible tells us, "Ye have not, because ye ask not." And, "If any of you lack wisdom, let him ask of God, that giveth to all men liberally."

God enables the natural women to do the supernatural. He uses the ordinary women to accomplish the extraordinary. He can convert her woman's intuition into something holy and sensible. With a woman's teachable spirit, He can produce creative, spiritual energy, perception, and balanced emotion.

A woman who can make people feel good naturally, who combines her faith with holy intuition, will dig out the answers to personal and world problems.

As I see it, we are not human beings, we are human *becomings*, a Church on the way, not arrived . . . ever praying, ever learning. God doesn't *choose* royalty, He *develops* it!

Come with me as I share what God has taught me about living in harmony—through prayer, through our relationships, through our health, through a sense of humor, and through simplicity.

WOMEN
IN TUNE

1

In Tune with God

"May the God of peace . . . work in us what is pleasing to him."

Hebrews 13:20–21, NIV

At my house every morning is like Easter. As I lie in bed, I visualize the death of one day and the rising up of another. The darkness of the air, the darkness of my sleep, my buried body— lying prone on a comfortable bed and covered by blankets—all symbolize the demise of yesterday, along with its disappointments and mistakes.

Before I uncover my body I think about the rising sun and the light that is announcing the dawn of a new day. As I close the fingers of my left hand around the sheet-and-blanket shroud to throw it back, I make a fist with my right hand. As I lie on my back I greet the day by thrusting that right fist upward toward the ceiling and, with great gusto, declare, "Yes. Yes, Lord!" A sense of release tears through my rib cage. My breathing sets into its daytime rhythm, and I feel like a resurrected woman. I have told the Conductor of the orchestra of my life that this day is His. It frightens the devil to hear me say yes to the Lord, a positive first

17

word — even before a cup of coffee! He's too surprised to inject a negative thought.

Singer Lillie Knauls performs a song that prompted me to tune in to God in such a physical way. She sings "Every morning I say, Yes" and it's just what I've needed to get every day started right.

Before any orchestra begins a concert, all the members tune up to the note "A," which, in musical terms is defined as standard pitch 440. Every member of the orchestra must adjust his or her instrument so that it "lines up" with this tonal authority.

A small music group might ask one member to sound "A" on a pitch pipe so everyone could tune up with each other. A more professional group might take a pitch from a recently tuned piano. But for those who are very particular there is an access number in Fort Collins, Colorado, at the International Bureau of Standards (available through radio station WWV), where a person can hear pure "A," the authority by which music is judged to be in or out of tune.

They also have a clock there that is accurate to a billionth of a second. You may check this authority to be "in tune" with time.

In his book *Riding the Wind*, Terry Fullam mentions a trip he took to Brazil. While there, he listened to the country's most powerful radio station, which happens to be operated by the Pentecostal Church. From one end of that huge country to the other, this station beams music and Scripture readings, but it also has two other prime functions that serve to keep people in tune who live deep in the jungle: Three minutes out of every ten the station announces the correct time; then, twice a day, the musical note "A" is broadcast for one or two minutes. Music is important to the Brazilians and they value the importance of staying on course, in tune.

A Backward Look

There's nothing new about staying in tune with God. Women said yes to Him long before science understood how sound and pitch worked.

The Bible is full of accounts of men and women who were tuned in to God's voice and who said yes to Him. Luke 1 tells two parallel stories: A man, Zacharias, and a woman, Mary, are both visited by an angel. Let's look at the two stories and see who is more tuned in.

Zacharias, an old man married to an old and barren woman, is given a hard-to-believe message by an angel. His wife, Elizabeth, will conceive and bear a son. Zacharias hears the words but can't make sense of them. No. Elizabeth's womb has dried up. It's not physically possible. So he asks the angel, Gabriel, for proof. "Whereby shall I know this? for I am an old man, and my wife well stricken in years" (Luke 1:18). Gabriel gives Zacharias a sign: He is stricken dumb for more than nine months, until after the baby is born. But Gabriel acknowledges that he's giving this sign "because thou believest not my words, which shall be fulfilled in their season" (verse 20).

Now let's look at Mary. The angel's words to her also concern the coming of a baby. He says that Mary, a virgin, will conceive—with no help from a man.

In my view, this message is harder to believe than Zacharias's, yet Mary has a different response. Amazed, she asks how it will take place. Gabriel explains that the Holy Spirit will come upon her; her son will be the "Son of God." What does she say? As I

19

would paraphrase it she says, "Yes, Lord. I'm Your woman, and I believe what You say." She didn't ask for proof but rather recognized truth and responded to truth when she heard it.

We all make choices, decide to say yes or no. And, of course, much of our "success" in life depends on saying yes to the right requests—God's requests. I believe that if we are responding to God's call we will know our yeses are right. We will have the peace and joy that only He can give—no matter what the circumstances are around us. For instance, the circumstances around Mary's decision must have been very difficult. Even her beloved Joseph questioned her purity until God told him the truth of it. We can only imagine the reception she must have gotten as friends and neighbors discovered she was pregnant out of wedlock.

But Mary had said yes to God and in her heart was peace. Look at these beautiful words she spoke to her cousin Elizabeth: "My soul praises the Lord and my spirit rejoices. . . . From now on all generations will call me blessed, for the Mighty One has done great things for me—holy is his name" (Luke 1:46–48, NIV). Mary did not look around her, she looked to God and found her peace in His approval.

When we are in tune and say yes to God's call we will know the peace that passes all comprehension—a peace only those who have shared it will understand.

Think about the circumstances of your life and the times you have said yes to God. It can be an encouragement as you see the evidence of His hand on your life. Here is a sampling of the yeses I recall in my life, the times I moved forward in the flow of God's Spirit.

When I was eight years old, I bought a nineteen-cent tablet with four sections, pink, blue, yellow, and green. I would sit in the back seat of my dad's old Hudson with my brothers while our family drove the thirteen miles from our farm in Terre Haute, Indiana, to a little red brick church my dad pastored in Clinton. One Sunday morning one brother asked, "What are you always doing, writing and scribbling?" I told him, "I'm going to be a writer." My brothers hooted. But their reaction didn't change my dream. Although the dream would lie dormant for years, I never forgot that day when I said yes to being a writer.

When I was thirteen I said yes to Jesus. I knew I was a sinner in need of a Savior. I wanted Him to live within me and make my heart clean as new-fallen snow.

My dad asked me to say yes to music so I could help the church by singing and playing the organ. At age eleven I strapped an accordion to my chest and played for jail services and nursing homes. I must have put 12,000 miles on it before my father took a pastorate in New Castle, Indiana. My parents moved and I stayed with Uncle Jesse and Aunt Gertrude so I wouldn't have to change schools my senior year. After I graduated I joined my family in New Castle. The first Sunday there, I met John and two years later said yes to him at the church altar.

John and I moved to Florida and looked for a large, exciting church to attend, but we settled into a small one in Palm Harbor that needed an organist—and an organ. I said yes, moved my own organ into the sanctuary, and played it for eight years.

In 1959 I said yes to life itself. I'd been in a coma for forty-four days when I died—literally. I left this world and saw Jesus standing in a golden throne room. I saw people who had died before me—happy and healthy. They knew me and I knew them! And then I became aware of my father's prayers. After being dead for twenty-eight minutes, I opened my eyes in my hospital room. Two days later I went home—with no discernible physical difficulties caused by my original ailment, an appendix that had ruptured eleven days before and gangrene that had spread throughout my abdomen.

Two years later my husband, John, died, five weeks after undergoing open heart surgery. I was pregnant with our second daughter and was torn between saying yes to the realities of widowhood and yes to the joys of motherhood.

Six years later I said yes to a man I met in the express lane of a grocery store. He was a returned missionary with three children; his wife had died of cancer. Saying yes to Carl also meant saying yes—eventually—to being a pastor's wife.

I never wanted to be a pastor's wife. We moved to Pasadena, Texas, where Carl took a church. When a deacon first handed me a key and said, "Would you like to see the parsonage?" I replied softly, "No." He thought I was spiritually mature when I said, "If the pulpit fits my husband, the parsonage will fit me." But actually I was digging in my heels. I did not voice my opinion, but started saying, "Yes, Lord," again even though it was hard. The Lord verified the importance of saying yes to Him. When I did, the congregation grew 400%. I developed lifetime friendships there, but I yearned to return "home," to the prairies that I'd learned suited me best.

When we moved back to the Dakotas I said yes to the editor of the *Dickey County Leader* who asked me to write a weekly column of candid musings, "Betty's Bits." At last, that dream as a child to be a writer was coming to fruition.

Carl became vice-president of Trinity Bible College in Ellendale, North Dakota. A student there asked if he could write the story of my death experience for a journalism class. He sent some copies of it to his friends, and a relative of his sent one on to Catherine Marshall. Her husband, Len LeSourd, asked me to write a book. That was the first of five. In middle age I said yes to a writing career. Life *can* begin at forty!

The proof that we are in tune with God is the "living proof"— love, joy, peace, longsuffering, gentleness, meekness, goodness, faith, and temperance. I can see now how the Lord helped me through the hard times and gave me many joyous times as well, always guiding me into a more finely tuned relationship, for which I'll be eternally grateful.

Being Out of Tune

Do you remember the game "Gossip" that children play at parties? You sit in a circle and the leader whispers into the ear of the person on her right a sentence, soft and fast. Then that person hurries and whispers to the one on her right, around the circle. At the end, the last person announces what she heard. The farther from the source, the more distorted, out-of-focus, out-of-tune, the message. Just so, the farther we are from the Source of the message, the more discordant our lives.

A friend, Paul Hamelink, mentioned an experiment made by a friend of his. He took a 33 1/3-rpm recording of a fine symphony orchestra, and he drilled a hole that was an eighth of an inch off-center. The result? When he played the record that wonderful music turned into something *weird*. When the polar center was even slightly off-center, the music became eccentric— which *means* off-center.

Because Adam and Eve chose to be disobedient, we all start life off-center or out-of-tune. At birth, I believe each baby is plugged in, equipped with a conscience that will sustain him or her until the age of accountability. But then each person must voluntarily choose whether or not to plug in to God's Son, Jesus.

God's desire is to bring everyone above the age of accountability (whatever that may be) into perfect alignment with His perfect pitch, and that's what He does when we say yes to His salvation. But many people say yes to counterfeit truths that only make their lives more discordant, before they respond to the strong, steady voice of God.

Many of us want a face change, some a name change, but we all need a heart change, a heart that pants after God like the deer pants after the water (see Psalm 42:1).

Listening to God

As a small child I had a poster on my bedroom wall with a little phosphorous luminous cross on it. It lightened the darkness only after it had been exposed to light. In some ways, you and I are like that cross. We can't absorb *or* reflect God's light and truth—we can't stay in tune with Him—unless we are exposed to His light and truth, His perfect tone.

William Arthur said, "If you would have your soul surcharged with the fire of God so that everyone who comes near you will know you are in tune with the Almighty and feel some mysterious influence proceeding out from you, you must draw near the source of that fire and power to the throne of God and of the Lamb. Shut yourself in from that cold world which so swiftly steals our warmth. Enter into your closet, shut the door and there isolated before the throne await the Baptism; then the fire will fill you and when you come forth, Holy Power will accompany you and you will no longer labor in your own strength but in demonstration of the Holy Spirit and God's power."

Proverbs 8:17 says of wisdom, "Those that seek me early shall find me." I'm an early riser and the first hour of my day, spent with my Lord, is invaluable to my spiritual well-being. I open His Word and drink in His message to me. I listen to His voice within my Spirit. I absorb Him.

I like to think that Jesus' mother, Mary, was one of the women who rose early, before sunrise, on Easter morning to go and tend to the body of their Lord. It seems as if they couldn't wait to be with Him, even if it was only His dead body they were expecting to find.

When they took the effort to get up and go into His presence, they were stunned by the surprise, the blessing He had in store for them. Mary Magdalene was among these women, and John 20 says that Jesus appeared to her outside His tomb and talked to her as if they were old friends. At first she didn't recognize Him; she mistook Him for a gardener. But when she saw the truth of the moment, she gasped, "Master." She saw and recognized—and said yes to—the Lord's glory.

When I rise early in the morning to spend time with God, I ask Him to show me His glory. I expect to see His glory, to receive His blessing, to hear His perfectly pitched tone. And God does speak—through the general promises of the Word, and also straight to the heart. We must wait. We must tarry, and follow Jesus' word to abide in Him, but He does speak.

My friend Sara Douglas is a quiet, reserved woman of prayer. Each summer she used to visit with a friend in Asheville, North Carolina, who had a deep spiritual need. For years Sara had unsuccessfully tried to help her friend resolve her inner conflicts. Then one morning while Sara was praying for this friend, a name kept coming to mind. Sara checked a phone directory and learned it was the name of a minister in Asheville. She called and explained her strange impulse to the pastor. He responded by visiting Sara's friend who heard the truth of his words and confessed her personal and spiritual need.

God does speak to those who listen, but I'm the first to admit that too many people are looking for magic and their personal gurus.

Far too many egotists are professing to be religious palm-readers and Christian fortune-tellers. Because of this I'm hesitant to receive messages that come from God secondhand, though I've discovered He sometimes speaks this way.

One day in the mail I received a letter from a woman containing only three sentences. "Betty, In prayer I felt God wanted me to send you a message. It is Proverbs 24:14d, 'Thy expectation shall not be cut off.' May He reveal the hidden meaning to you."

I thought it was nice, read it again, then placed it in the wastepaper basket. That afternoon when I was packing for a trip to Indianapolis, Indiana, to speak for a woman's prayer conference, I felt prompted to retrieve the letter and put it in my briefcase.

Later during my opening remarks, I couldn't seem to get going. The words I had chosen to use for greeting had evaporated. I had a mental block. All I could think of was the letter. I explained how I had acquired it. I read it, and then I proceeded with my planned topic. That letter had an amazing impact on the rest of the weekend. I am still getting letters from participants who, from that woman's action, were stirred in faith to receive the miracle they needed. Those responses indicate that women are continuing to get answers to prayer according to their willingness to say yes to God.

Faith, I've learned, is sanctified imagination.

An artist, Adelle Waddington, was doing some illustrations for me. One day she brought her four-year-old daughter over and sent her out to play while we worked. Some time later the child came in, red-faced, sweaty, and tired.

"What have you been doing?" the young mother asked.

"Playing ball with God," the girl replied. "I throw the ball up to God and He always throws it back to me, even if I don't catch it!" Now that's imaginative faith. This child had a real assurance of God's presence.

And God *is* with us; that is exactly what the name Immanuel means—"God with us, revealed *in us.*" We can stand on the Word that promises, "I will instruct thee and teach thee in the way which thou shalt go." The more I become one with God, the more I know the sound of His voice, the more I understand the receiving from above. It is not good to believe every impression that comes; our nudgings ought to be pondered and considered advisedly and leisurely so that God Almighty will not be offended through our fickleness. Just because a woman has one divine impulse doesn't mean that all her future impulses are divine. We have to keep in tune to make sure that what we're hearing is God's voice, which always lines up with the perfect truth of His Word.

God calls us into solitude to strengthen us. Alone, we get in tune with ourselves and the Holy Spirit builds us up; He gives divine tone, color, and resourcefulness to our spirit. Put yourself at peace in the presence of God; then you may better make others at peace.

I'm obviously a proponent of early morning "tuning in" sessions. The Old Testament says that the prophet Daniel knelt toward Jerusalem and prayed three times a day (6:10). If you remember the story, he landed in the lions' den. He was so in tune with God that even starved lions were afraid to eat him!

Three times a day is an effective prayer pattern, but the apostle Paul suggests an even more challenging one. In 1 Thessalonians 5:17 he says, "Pray without ceasing." I listen to God throughout the whole day—as I drive, as I ride my bicycle, as I sit in church, as I watch television, while I'm on the floor doing my back exercises, as I'm reaching out to others.

What effect does this "tuning in" have on my daily life? I can hear God's nudges. I can reflect on and time-test the words I hear Him speak to my spirit. I can move as He directs me.

Last week on a day that was already too full I needed to see the newspaper editor, Rodger Biggs, and give a prayer article to one of the college professors, Sam Brelo. But God was orchestrating my day. When I was thirsty, I got up and got a drink at the kitchen sink. When I looked out the kitchen window I saw Rodger Biggs, who "just happened" to be passing by. Later, I was almost late for chapel, but as I pulled into the parking lot, who should walk behind my car but Sam Brelo! There are many advantages to *staying in tune* with God.

They say that anything you do thirty-five times becomes a habit. That means that in just a month you can be a success by automatically saying yes to God every morning—and praying throughout your day.

What a way to frighten the devil and get the bluff on him! Satan doesn't care if you talk about him or mean-mouth him just as long as he can prevent you from *talking to God*. He would seek to short-circuit your lifeline, or unplug you from the source and solution to *all* life's issues. But prayer is the one weapon Satan doesn't have. He is no match for you and God. Keep in tune!

Talking to God

I was taught to pray when I was two. I learned to pray when I was forty-two. While playing tennis with neighbors I reprimanded Chuck for his terrible language. "You must watch your profanity," I said. "Your two little girls are picking up on it. I'm going to pray for you about this."

Leaning against the net, Chuck grinned, looked straight at me, and said, "Aw, Betty, I cuss a lot, you pray a lot. And neither one of us really means what we're saying." I felt as if he had struck a blow between my eyes with a sledge hammer.

I started a prayer journey that afternoon and I'm still learning.

The lesson was reinforced a few days later when I was struggling over my weekly newspaper column. I needed but couldn't come up with a fresh idea. Right then the phone rang. One of my brothers—who is a clown—was on the line. We chatted for a minute and then he said, "I have a great idea for your column. Why don't you do one on how Americans waste words?" He explained how he got the idea. He was walking across a parking lot and encountered a small old woman, frowning and carrying a heavy sack of groceries. He said politely, "Good morning. How are you?" And with a snarl she snapped, "Constipated." He was surprised that he got a straight answer, and realized he hadn't really wanted such an honest response. He had used all those words when he had just meant to relay a simple "Hello." We agreed that we do waste words, and say things without meaning them.

I used that incident as the basis of my column and felt glad that I could share a timely—and humorous—story with my readers.

On the way home from the newspaper office Chuck's comment on the tennis court struck home again. Wasting words in idle conversation was one thing; wasting words in prayer was a travesty. How many times did I let my mind wander . . . What should I wear to the noon luncheon? Then I'd pull myself back: "I'm sorry, Lord, I'm supposed to be praying." But in a few minutes it would happen again . . . Did I take anything out of the freezer for dinner?

Who was I kidding? No wonder my prayers were not being answered. God was too busy running the universe to shift into neutral while I dabbled with trivial things. On that October morning I dropped onto my knees in front of a black leather chair and got serious about prayer. I made a pact with God: "Lord, when You see me kneel or bow my head or hear me speak Your name, You can know that I mean business. I will say what I mean and mean what I say. I won't waste Your time or mine. I won't let my mind wander. I'll concentrate on what I am praying. I will remember who You are, Holy Deity, if You will give me answers to my prayers."·

How do we talk to God? By shutting out distractions and talking to Him straight, on a "private line." Nothing is beyond the reach of prayer except that which lies outside of the will of God. No woman accomplishes so much in so little time as when she is praying.

Mary Queen of Scots was more afraid of the prayers of John Knox than she was of the armies of Europe. When Jesus decided to change His Father's world, He called together twelve simple men. He didn't even teach them to preach; He taught them to pray.

I have a brand-new computer in my writing studio. I hate that thing! Every time I look at it I think I will throw up. Do you know why? Because I don't know how it works. I have not had time to learn about it, but those who do understand its principles tell me that I'll love it once I learn. It's the same with prayer. When we understand how prayer works, we'll love praying.

How does it work? James 4:2 tells us, "Ye have not, because ye ask not." When you pray, don't try to formulate, speculate, dictate, or manipulate the Lord. His ways are past finding out. God has a thousand ways to work when I cannot see one, and when all *my* means have reached their end, then *His* have just begun.

You may ask, "What if I pray wrong?"

When I want to express something in legal terms, I need an attorney. When I write a book I need an editor. When I pray to the Father in Jesus' name, Jesus, my Advocate, my Attorney, takes my pitiful attempt at prayer, refines it through His filtering system according to my motive, and presents it in its purest form to the Father. That's why we get answers even though we may pray a shabby prayer.

After we have reached the Holy Spirit, we can pray in the Spirit, letting Him pray through us. Satan cannot intercept or prevent our petitioning.

God hears every prayer you pray after that initial prayer, "Lord, be merciful to me, a sinner." Then, when you pray "Father, in the name of Jesus," you have an immediate audience with the Almighty. Your prayers go directly to that golden throne room where Jesus is at the right hand of the Father, where thousands and thousands of angels are waiting for the Crew Dispatcher, the Personnel Manager, the King of the angels—Jesus—to signal them to go into the world and bring an answer to your prayer.

A saintly widow I know watched as her daughter slipped into

an ungodly lifestyle, being influenced by undesirable friends. She prayed earnestly that God would keep the girl from harm. The mother knew she couldn't be with the girl every hour and asked God to be her guardian.

One night the girl and another young woman won the chance to go backstage and meet (and presumably spend the night with) a singing group performing at a disco known as a center for drug distribution and prostitution. They knocked at the door excitedly, but a woman with pitch-black hair eyed them suspiciously for a few moments. Finally she spoke. "You can go in," she said to the friend, but she pointed to my friend's daughter and said, "You can't come in here."

The rejected girl yelled, "I have a right to be here. Why are you trying to stop me?"

The doorkeeper told her an amazing thing. "I am a witch," she said, "a fortune-teller. Just now I saw two angels, one on each side of you. I dare not let you in here."

As the stunned girl told her mother this story later, my friend rejoiced that God had answered her prayers. She came to Him in prayer from then on with a heart full of thanksgiving, as well as intercession.

Anything large enough for a wish to light upon is worth hanging a prayer upon.

There is a prayer that asks for nothing, yet asks for everything. If you seek the Father in Jesus' name you are likely to receive what you ask for and more.

You may be locked into a dead marriage or a dull job. You may be nursing a dream that has died. You may have done everything right and still have gone-wrong kids. You may have climbed the ladder of success only to find it leaning against the wrong wall. Just try the experiment of saying yes and tuning in to God every morning. Find quiet time to listen and talk to God and plug into the power of the Holy Spirit. Remember, Jesus is "the same, yesterday, today and forever." He is still resurrecting and breathing power into us!

Every morning can be Easter at your house—as it is at mine.

2

In Tune with Others

"Freely ye have received, freely give."

Matthew 10:8

I'm an investment expert. Let me explain.

One night before falling asleep I told my husband, "I wanna be rich. I'm tired of being poor."

"Go ahead," he said. "You've got my permission. Fame or fortune, if it happens to you, it happens to me; we have the same last name!"

As fate would have it, two days later a man rang our doorbell and said, "Some of your friends suggested that I stop by. I already have three other couples interested, and if you would like to invest, we will sink an oil well in Kentucky—and all get rich."

You probably won't believe that we actually decided to take part in such a shaky scheme, but I was determined to think big. We took all we had out of savings, we sold our older, second car, and we invested.

Three weeks later we heard exhilarating news. "Come quick,"

34

the voice on the phone said. "We've got a gusher! It's already pumped eighty barrels today!"

We drove fast, found the site, and stood enrapt while that black stuff spewed and sprayed us. We didn't care what we looked like. It felt so good to be filthy rich.

That night we went to a nearby (cheap) motel, but we couldn't fall asleep. We were too excited. We didn't need to sleep to enjoy our dreams. We were like children on Christmas Eve—"nestled all snug in our beds, while visions of sugar plums danced in our heads."

I said, "No more self-serve gas pumps for me." My husband said, "I'm sick of those little dinky motel soap bars you bring home from trips. Now we'll buy full-sized bars." Our daughter chimed in, "And I'm tired of using that cheap scraper paper. Can we buy White Cloud toilet tissue?" We decided our collie dogs had gagged on generic dog food long enough. Now they would dine on Alpo. We would make a missions pledge at church. I would have my back teeth filled—instead of just the front ones. I would replace my worn underwear, instead of being concerned only with my outer wear. We rolled in bed laughing. I thought of a little old woman in our town whom everyone called Grandma Rice. She had a quote, "Tell me what thou hast need of and I will tell thee how thou canst get along without it." Wouldn't she have something to say if she had seen us that night!

A couple days later we came back down to earth and went home to work for a living.

Two weeks later the balloon burst. The phone rang. Our gusher had dwindled to a dribble. The rig was pulled, the equipment returned, and the labor crew let go.

When the venture was over our net profit was $2.34. I didn't even cash the check. I framed it.

We didn't learn our lesson. We invested in two acres of Florida property. We built a house on it and then sold it—for exactly what we had in it.

We bred and sold registered quarter horses and collies, but never showed a profit. Of course, we benefited from good, wholesome family time, but money? No.

During my widow years, I tried United Funds. But when my car caught fire and I learned that the auto insurance had run out four days previously, I went to the bank to cash in the Funds—which were at an all-time low.

It's not that I didn't know better, I had gotten the message—a message clearer to me than anything on earth—that I was to make a different kind of investment my priority, I realized sheepishly my *sole* priority. I received that message during the twenty-eight minutes I was clinically dead and walked up a green hill into the magnificent city of heaven. There I recalled a common phrase, "You can't take it with you." I realized that the only earthly investment that has any value in heaven is *people*.

Now, there was no condemnation in that wonderful place. But I sensed that if I stayed there I would be given no reward. I knew myself. I had never really liked people unless they could promote my well-being or contribute something to me. Oh, how I wished for a second chance to live again, to love again. I got it, and this time around I'm learning to invest in people, and I've become rich. She is rich who is satisfied . . . .

If you will invest in people, God will endorse your program and you will be a success. What is success? It's finding a need and filling it.

I spoke at a state bankers' convention where I heard newscaster Dan Rather speak. He told us that he printed a message to himself on three cards that he then placed in prominent places where he sees them throughout each day. The cards say: "What are you doing right now that will affect the broadcast?" I went home and printed myself three cards. I put one in my purse, one in my car, and one on my desk. They say, "Invest in people." I never want to forget that people are more important than things.

The Bible makes it clear that we are not saved by our works. Ephesians 2:8–9 says, "For by grace are ye saved through faith; and that not of yourselves: it is the gift of God: Not of works, lest any man should boast." But the very next verse says that we are "created in Christ Jesus unto good works, which God hath before ordained that we should walk in them."

James, Jesus' brother, said, "Faith without works is dead," but Paul, in 1 Corinthians 13, tells us what the good works must be built on: a foundation of love. "Though I bestow all my goods to feed the poor, and though I give my body to be burned, and have not charity, it profiteth me nothing." That's exactly what I learned at the gates of heaven. All my good works up to that point would have profited me nothing because I hadn't properly invested in people—by loving them, by being in tune with them and their needs.

I get nervous when I hear a soloist say, "I love to sing," or a minister comment, "I love to preach," even a teacher admit that she "loves to teach." But when I hear individuals declare they love the people they sing to, preach to, or teach, I smile, knowing they are on the right track with the right motive. God created people, Jesus died for people, and the Holy Spirit is still indwelling people.

Now God isn't expecting us to do something He hasn't already done. God Himself is love (1 John 4:8). He invested His creative energy to create Adam and Eve and in turn all of humanity. He sent His Son here to earth to become one of us. His whole life—

and death—can be summarized with the word *love*. There's a description of Jesus' ministry hidden away in Acts 10:38. Peter is presenting the Gospel to a Gentile, Cornelius, and Peter says that Jesus "went about doing good."

Meeting Needs

That's a one-line summary. If you took a few hours and read any one of the four Gospels, you'd see a pattern in Jesus' ministry: He gravitated toward need. When He called Matthew, a tax collector, to be one of His disciples, the Pharisees asked why He associated with sinners. He had a quick and perfect answer, "It is not the healthy who need a doctor, but the sick" (Matthew 9:12, NIV). Then He immediately challenged them to action. He said, "But go and learn what this means: 'I desire mercy, not sacrifice.' " And the Pharisees would have known that He was quoting from the Old Testament, Hosea 6:6.

The "establishment" didn't always like the fact that Jesus reached out to sinners, and in some regards that's still true.

When you really tune in to need, you may get out of tune with certain people. At one of the churches Carl pastored I was trying hard to be a good pastor's wife. Every Tuesday night I went to the women's meeting and struggled to keep interested in the hand projects the older women were working on. One week I excused myself and said I wouldn't be able to attend; I had an appointment with a needy woman.

Well, the following morning, one "Sainted Sally" called two others and they appointed "Mollie Missionary" to report the pastor's wife to the pastor—my husband. She let him know that those four knew I hadn't attended the circle because I had been riding around town in a silver Lincoln Continental with a wealthy woman who was an alcoholic, who neglected her children, and who was unfaithful to her husband.

When Carl told me what he'd heard, I did what any mature woman would do. I called my father and cried. He listened and then calmly said, "Maturity is to suffer without complaining, and be misunderstood without explaining." Now I didn't mind being misunderstood if they would let me explain, give me my day in court. But I kept quiet.

Two months later at the Tuesday night circle this former alcoholic, poor mother, bad wife, wept as she told the women that I had jeopardized my reputation to be seen with her, that I had prayed with her, and that the steering wheel of her Lincoln Continental had been the altar at which she had wept as Jesus had washed away her sins. She explained that she never would have been seen dead in our church. She had needed someone to come to her, where she was. I looked around and saw that the critical quartet was weeping. When they found out how rewarding it is to serve, many women in that circle left the quilting to the older women and set out to rescue the perishing and lift up the fallen, so that the broken strings of their lives could vibrate harmoniously once more.

Our Circle Is Too Small

One November I rented a car and fought my way through evening rush hour traffic in downtown New Orleans, trying to get to a church on Airline Highway where I was to speak at 6:30. I couldn't believe the traffic. My knuckles were white, I was grabbing the steering wheel so tightly. I was desperately praying that I would not get killed by the crazy drivers who were determined to get somewhere—fast. I noticed that even the new cars around me, that year's models, were banged and mangled. And the taxis, well, you couldn't even tell what make they were, just that they were yellow or black and white checkered. I was overwhelmed with the frantic pace.

God truly ministered to me—and through me—in that evening service. The Lord seemed to remind me of how narrow my Midwestern lifestyle is. He had confronted me with city life for a purpose; I had too tightly hung onto my dream of living in the tranquil countryside—germ free, people free, taxi free—refusing to see *need* on a large scale level.

Before I spoke, a soloist sang, "I'm going to stop this hauling water to the sea, but carry the water to the desert." And that's what God helped me speak on that night. I said, "Tonight Jesus is here to gravitate toward your need, to resurrect your faith and bring back alive your lost hope!" I knew the Holy Spirit was speaking through me.

When I finished thirty-eight people came down the aisle weeping to beg forgiveness for sin and to receive the passport to eternity and to walk here on the earth as new creatures, not good as new, but *all new*. The last four who came were prostitutes who had been sitting back under the balcony. They were cleansed, washed clean.

What happened that night reminds me of this haunting poem by George MacDonald:

> I said, "Let me walk in the field."
>   God said, "Nay, walk in the town."
> I said, "There are no flowers there."
>   He said, "No flowers, but a crown."
> I said, "But the sky is black,
>   there is nothing but noise and din."

But he wept as he sent me back,
"there is more," he said, "there is sin."

I said, "But the air is thick,
and fogs are veiling the sun."
  He answered, "Yet souls are sick,
  And souls in the dark undone."
I said, "I shall miss the light,
and friends will miss me, they say."
  He answered me, "Choose tonight,
  If I am to miss you, or they."

I pleaded for time to be given.
  He said, "Is it hard to decide?
  It will not seem hard in Heaven,
  to have followed the steps of your Guide."
I cast one look at the fields,
then set my face to the town.
  He said, "My child, do you yield?
  Will you leave the flowers for a crown?"

Then, into His hand went mine,
  and into my heart came He;
And I walk in a light Divine,
  the path I had feared to see.

When Carl was a missionary in Egypt, he walked along a main road in the middle of one afternoon. He noticed a group of eight men watching him and whispering. He stopped to chat with them and eventually asked, "Why were you whispering?"

One man spoke out honestly. "The last missionary had an air-conditioned automobile. We know his car. You have no car, so we know your face. You walk with us, talk with us."

Carl was profoundly touched by those words.

How many people in the U.S. travel to a cathedral in an

expensive air-conditioned car to *learn how* to invest in people, but pass hundreds on the way who need to know them and their Jesus?

Most of our Christian friends are overexposed to good teaching. We keep vaccinating the same people over and over again against sin and judgment.

Last year a poll was taken, showing 7,000 churches that didn't win a single soul in a year. That is 560,000 sermons, dry runs— what expensive wasted time and labor!

And we can't blame their hardness of heart on the needy. Are we active in the church, or active for God? The needy know the difference in a "teacher"—who loves to preach, expound, and teach—and a concerned woman of prayer. But we must evangelize or fossilize.

Many churches are religious clubs of pampered pets. We are loaded down with religious activity and Christian socials.

Too many women can weep and look gravely concerned, but are more pretty than practical, more fancy than functional. We are spoiled by good things like film negatives ruined from overexposure to the light. I still need to build up my faith by worshiping with praising people, but I have determined to quit hob-knobbing with Christian snobs. We keep building each other up, pumping each other, teaching the deeper life. We already know too much. The wrung-out woman is usually in tune with tapes, music, books; none of these will revive her, will deepen her life so rapidly as seeing one soul saved.

There's something radically wrong with group meetings planned just to provide participants with a good old spiritual "hoe down." I attended a women's meeting in the Midwest that should have been submitted to the *Guinness Book of World Records*. Each woman preached a little more until it became a competitive game of "can you top this?" We were dismissed at 12:04—that means midnight.

Second Timothy 3 contains some interesting phrases: "In the last days . . . men shall be lovers of their own selves . . . lovers of pleasures more than lovers of God; Having a form of godliness, but denying the power thereof: from such turn away (verses 1–2, 4–5).

Let's reverse this Scripture: Some have the form of power but deny the godliness thereof, from such turn away. I would call some of these groups I've attended Charismatic Critics of Acrobatic Liturgists. They would stick up their noses at "formal" churches because their liturgy is dead, but they don't see that their own worship is habitual and hollow. Charismata without character produce chaos. They're not reaching out to people in need nor up to God with heartfelt prayers. The purpose of prayer is not to impress people, but to invest in them, in their needs.

Sometimes our pray-ers are spectators always studying the sport of prayer, but not actually wrestling and practicing what they're learning. In Ephesians 6:12–20 Paul says that "our struggle is not against flesh and blood, but against the rulers, against the authorities, against the powers of this dark world and against the spiritual forces of evil in the heavenly realms . . ." (NIV). He goes on to describe the armor we Christians are to wear and he ends the passage with: "Be alert and always keep on praying for all the saints. Pray also for me, that whenever I open my mouth, words may be given me so that I will fearlessly make known the mystery of the gospel. . . . Pray that I may declare it fearlessly, as I should."

He takes seriously his call to invest in people and he asks that the Ephesians also wake up to the importance of the work.

Many people enjoy watching the game of life, but are not

willing to get off their bleachers, apply God and guts, and fight the warfare.

Beware that you do not traffic in unfelt truth . . . praying the same prayers, singing the same songs, quoting the same Scripture, engaging in religious ritual without tender feeling for people in their need. If you have a restless, melancholy heart, try gravitating toward need, praying for people, investing in them. People don't care how much you know, until they know how much you care.

Not for Praise

The needs around us are not always spiritual needs but often are physical. Whether you see a person straining in the miry clay of sin or the quicksand of deception, whether they are beached on the white sands of Florida, or snowbound in the Dakotas, move toward their personal needs and Jesus will help you satisfy their spiritual needs too. One friend Madge prays for me, but she shows her love in more concrete ways. She sends me pecans to cook with, and she once bought me a knit suit to wear for a telecast.

I saw too much truth in a cartoon I recently came across. It pictured a person looking from the balcony of a stain-glassed church onto the street below. The pitiful person in view begged, "I need love. My hands are cold." The voice from the balcony suggested, "Jesus loves you, and sit on your hands."

In Matthew 25:40 Jesus talks about meeting people's physical needs and He very pointedly said, "Inasmuch as ye have done it unto one of the least of these my brethren, ye have done it unto me." He's referring to meeting needs that sometimes we'd like to turn our backs on: visiting the sick and imprisoned, clothing and feeding the poor.

Carl and I were once royally hosted at the Sheraton Towers in New Orleans. As we registered, Carl remarked to the porter, "Looks like you have a full house."

"Yeah," he responded, "preacher convention."

This piqued Carl's curiosity. "Tell me something," he said. "Are preachers good tippers?"

The man grinned. "This weekend I've gotten a hundred 'Praise the Lords' and about twenty-two tracts." He went on, "I finally told this one fancy dude, Praise the Lords don't buy groceries!"

My husband was too embarrassed to tell the porter that he was an ordained minister, but you can be sure the man got a decent tip.

I see a lot of "pedestal love" and "cheap Jesus" floating around. Many who publicly pledge a healthy sum to the church turn around and are miserly with the waitress or are always trying to bum discounts from Christian businessmen struggling to make a living.

Jesus had a few words to say about this attitude, which He saw in the Pharisees. In Matthew 6 He says, "Be careful not to do your 'acts of righteousness' before men, to be seen by them. If you do, you will have no reward from your Father in heaven. So when you give to the needy, do not announce it with trumpets, as the hypocrites do in the synagogues and on the streets, to be honored by men. I tell you the truth, they have received their reward in full. But when you give to the needy, do not let your left hand know what your right hand is doing, so that your giving may be in secret. Then your Father, who sees what is done in secret, will reward you" (1–4, NIV).

I would like to challenge you to gravitate toward need—

anonymously. Look at these examples of what it can accomplish.

Six times a school teacher talked the skinny, scrawny dropout into going back to school. We don't know the teacher's name, but the student, Abraham Lincoln, became one of our most influential presidents.

A wino found a $1 bill in the gutter. He headed for the liquor store. Realizing it was Thanksgiving eve, he decided instead to buy the wooden bat in the pawn shop window. He took it to a nearby orphanage and gave it to a six-year-old boy he'd seen always batting rocks with sticks. The donor didn't even give his name, but the priest at the Catholic orphanage says the boy's name was Babe Ruth.

My father attributes his success pastoring a church in New Castle to Nova Clark, the custodian who spent every Sunday evening on her knees in the furnace room alone, praying while my dad preached. For a long time, we averaged eight people per service kneeling at the altar, surrendering their lives to Jesus.

Luke, the writer of Acts, briefly describes a woman who was important in the church at Joppa. If her name gives an insight into her personality, she must have been quite a woman. Her name was Dorcas, which means gazelle, and Luke says she "was always doing good and helping the poor." But Dorcas died and the other Christians in town, distraught at her passing, summoned Peter. I can imagine they gathered around him and said, "Peter, *do* something." They took him to the room where Dorcas was laid out and, says Luke, "All the widows stood around him, crying and showing him the robes and other clothing that Dorcas had made while she was still with them" (Acts 9:39, NIV).

Peter did do something. He asked all the women to leave the room. He got down on his knees and he prayed. Then he said, "Dorcas, get up." And she did.

The New Testament gives several accounts of Jesus and the apostles raising the dead—a few children, a few men—but Dorcas is the only woman specifically mentioned in this category. And what did the Holy Spirit see fit to have us remember about her? She was in tune with people's physical needs. First Corinthians 12 ends with an extended list of ministries, and there, alongside healing and working miracles, is the ministry of "helps"—Dorcas's calling. Whenever I think of Dorcas's story I connect it with Paul's statement in 2 Corinthians 9:7: "God loveth a cheerful giver."

That phrase surely describes the sharp young woman I watched washing church windows one day. I asked the pastor about her and he said, "Her husband is not a Christian, hates this church, and refuses to let her give a dime. She cleans the church without pay, and each week we give her a receipt for fifty dollars. She turns it in to their C.P.A. and they get a tax break—from donations of which her husband is totally unaware."

Bob Brenneman recently spoke at Trinity College's missions convention. He, his wife, and their three children had just returned from the mission field. I remember when he first arrived at Trinity as a student.

He was tall, lanky, and very shy. Yet we recognized a quiet quality. He wanted to be a missionary, he said, and he claimed Romans 15:20 for his goal. "I don't want to build upon another man's foundation, but I want to preach to people who have never heard."

Bob had another goal; he wanted a wife, but didn't seem to know how to get the ball rolling. Carl saw this and tried a little matchmaking.

Bob attended "Wings and Feet," an early morning prayer and jogging group that Carl heads. In the exercise group Carl noticed a quiet, attractive girl, Sherry, and he introduced her to Bob. They began running together, then running around together dating, then they married. Their first assignment was Teen Challenge in Chicago. They spent their honeymoon as house parents for nine alcohol and drug rehab cases. They've spent their married life serving God and investing in people.

But let me tell you a little more of Bob's story. How did he get through college? With the help of a few in-tune women. One woman who'd moved to North Dakota from a warm climate had saved money for a winter coat three different times. But each time she accumulated the funds, she anonymously applied them to Bob's school bill. Several teachers and students also invested in him anonymously. Then a young widow with a baby son came to Trinity. Her husband had been killed in Vietnam. She had put aside tithe on the insurance money waiting for God's direction as to how it should be used. She felt nudged to give that large sum to launch Bob and Sherry in their mission work. (Since then the donor has met and married a fine Christian man and they have a child of their own. Investing in people is a two-way street!)

God Directs, God Rewards

As we tune in to God, He tunes us in to people.

As we walk by faith and not by sight, God will give insight. If we gravitate toward need, God will gravitate toward us with the supply for that need. We can rely on Him.

Martin Luther said he prayed an hour each day for an ordinary day, but if he had an especially busy day planned he would spend a couple of extra hours in prayer at the start of it. Because he needed more of His energy, he had to stay a little longer at the fuel pump. A full tank for a full journey. Some of us are not overworked but underpowered. People who marvel us with what they do are people who stay at the pump a little longer.

Phillips Brooks said, "Do not pray for tasks equal to your powers. Pray for powers equal to your tasks."

Several months ago I became stale. Too much speaking, traveling, and writing. Yet I was still on the road. It was Sunday morning and I was in Phoenix. I had prepared what I thought was an impressive message to give in a large church there, but the Lord awakened me early—at 5:30—and rolled me out of bed onto my knees. He quietly spoke to my heart's chamber, "Lay aside your stale notes. I will give you a message as fresh as the morning news and as refreshing as the morning dew."

I suggested an alternative. "But the message I've prepared will impress these people."

He replied, "I didn't bring you here to impress them, but to invest in them." I pride myself in having my head screwed on straight and both feet on the ground, but I knew I must listen. I opened the Bible and was directed to Proverbs 8, which speaks of the durable riches of wisdom. Then I turned to Deuteronomy 8 where the children of Israel are reminded that God is the one who gave them the Promised Land; He is the one who made them wealthy.

That morning the Lord gave me a simple message: Our motives must always be tested by one measure: Are we tuning into people's needs? If that is where we put our creative abilities, our earning power will be energized and our eternal inheritance will be secure. If we get in tune with people, if we love and invest in people, we will become rich. The more we invest, the more interest we earn.

I've heard many stories of the effects of that Sunday service, but let me share one that shows how one generous woman was enriched.

She and another woman had invested in a Hallmark Gift and Card shop. She had a connection with a paper company and she sent me some padded mailing envelopes. I give away lots of books to prisoners and the terminally ill so this gift was a great boost to my mailing efforts. I thought it was a one-time gift—but she has periodically sent more for four years now.

Well, a year ago, all the shops in the mall where her store is located were broken into. That is all but hers. Three of nine bolts on the door had been removed, and no more. Perhaps an angel was guarding this woman's investment because she invests in people.

I know another woman, a professional musician, who gives all her proceeds from playing the organ for weddings and funerals to foreign missions. You'd be surprised how much more in demand she is than other musicians in the area.

Our giving motive should be love, but we can expect that God always rewards those who are in tune with the need of others. As Proverbs 11:24 says, "One man gives freely, yet gains even more; another withholds unduly, but comes to poverty."

You can't accept an assignment from God with a money motive.

For one book, I kept track of the hours I spent at the typewriter and then I compared it with my royalty checks. I made $2.10 per hour—less than minimum wage.

But I don't feel that my labors went unrewarded. I can't describe the joy and sense of fulfillment I receive when I open and read a letter from a person who has had a need met because God spoke through the words I've put down on paper. That reward makes up for the poor wages.

One young woman called from Britain: "I went to the pharmacy to buy sleeping pills to commit suicide," she said. "Instead I bought your book *Prayers That Are Answered.* You and your book saved my life. Jesus saved my soul!"

My books have had a measure of success. But I've learned a lot. When my editor read my first manuscript, he plainly told me, "This would sell about thirty copies . . . to your relatives. It rings with triumphalism. Have you never struggled or learned to cope with disappointment and to rebound?"

I went back and rewrote my manuscript. I wanted to write a book—not just so I could feel good when I saw my name on it—but to help remove people's fear of death. I wanted to show them that Jesus is the only passport to "forever." It sold, and I'm still writing because I learned to address people's needs. God is in tune with people who are in tune with people. That book is now in eighteen languages!

I am grateful for people who are sensitive, in tune to God and in turn in tune to need. Harold and Pat Kemp are just one example. They don't make a big splash, but operate a free, lending library from their home in Hallock, Minnesota. A few weeks ago, after a long trip in Canada doing day and night programs with 100 Huntley Street, I was drained. I hid in their attic room, uninterrupted, and slept ten hours straight. Once when I was short $25 on our house payment, I didn't whine to people, I just prayed. And wouldn't you know, God worked through the Kemps, who felt led to send us a check for $25.

Being Faithful

Some super-duper spirituals think you have to wait around for a telegram from heaven to begin investing in people. I love what Jeff Nelson, youth pastor at Trinity College, said once. I asked him how he knew he was called to be a missionary. He quickly replied, "I didn't wait for a call, I volunteered. Volunteer soldiers make much better fighters than draftees."

There are so many ways you can be in tune with people. I've known some people who would like to write a book—yet they never write a note or letter to comfort someone. And I also know young people who have developed a thriving writing career simply by writing, not books at first, but encouraging letters to kids of missionaries overseas.

Florence is a frail older woman who stayed at home, but she has a love for people. Her goal, she tells me, is to write a letter to everyone in her city, pointing them to Jesus' love and eternal life. She has disassembled the Canton, Ohio, phone book, and has progressed through the alphabet, up to the T's of the directory.

I started by writing letters and now when I autograph a book, I try to pray and be sensitive putting a note, a quote, or Scripture in the front page, and God has amazingly directed me to hit on personal needs that I didn't even know about.

I love the "always" people, admire the "in the meantime" people—you know, those who are always available, steady and dependable, to follow God's leading, whether toward a permanent-type ministry or a briefer calling to fulfill in whatever time is available. God puts a premium on the faithful, the constant. He rewards integrity. Staying power will win over fire power. God is faithful to us (see Lamentations 3:23, "Great is thy faithfulness"); in turn, we are to be faithful even if it means we are not being noticed by other people.

For my daughter April's high school graduation, I took her to

the 1984 Summer Olympics in Los Angeles. We met Madelyn
Manning Mims, a former gold-medal runner. She told April,
"God will build you a platform if you love people and will
proclaim Jesus from it."

When I asked Marcia Kendall, founder of Flame Fellowship,
how the international organization started, she said she had had
a great desire to serve people. She sought the Lord about how she
could minister, and she thought God would give her a magnificent title and a powerful public assignment. But he kept
whispering to her spirit, "You will be a door opener for other
women." So she started begging her husband, John, for a bigger
house so she could work for the Lord ministering hospitality. He,
being the practical man he is, pointed out, "You aren't using the
little house you have." They started there, and God has since
given them an adequate, spacious home. The public ministry
finally came, but in the meantime, God used Marcia's willing
spirit and faithfulness. Take some people away from the microphone and they are nothing—not Marcia.

Great things are a combination of little things. Every action of
your life touches on some chord that will vibrate into eternity.

I pay tribute to my first husband, John. When we were first
married, he wanted to invite home for dinner a young couple
having marital problems. They both had been married before
and had brought the same psychological baggage into the second
marriage that they'd taken into the first ones. I dragged my feet.
I did not want them to come for fear people would think I was
endorsing their lifestyle. I have since learned that people don't
need to be reminded when they have erred. But John was years
ahead of me in his awareness of other people. He was not a
minister or counselor, just a man in tune with people and their
need. I'd watch, amazed as he'd wipe runny noses of children

with one hand as he filled a car's gas tank with the other. He'd do this for free for unemployed people looking for work.

If you invest in others, for God, for souls, the Lord will extend your credit and credibility with the Great Resource Bank.

Investing with Prayer

Esther Zink is the head librarian at Trinity College. She and her husband team-teach a couples' class, the Ellendale Breakfast Club, on Sunday morning; she's a prayer warrior; whether on the phone or on the street, she's an instant volunteer, in tune with need and reality. She says that intercessory prayer is "love on its knees."

Through prayer it is possible to transfer energy to the ministry or to the aid of another person. I know a young woman who is confined to a wheelchair because of rheumatoid arthritis. She can no longer play concert piano as she once did. But every morning she fervently and diligently prays for another concert pianist she knows, that God will energize and anoint him as he practices his piano. Every evening right after dinner, she wheels herself into her bedroom and prays that the Holy Spirit will inspire him that evening as he plays in concert—in whatever city he is scheduled to perform. I do not understand the concept of prayer power, but I believe in the transfer of love and energy from one person to another through prayer.

Another woman recently told me how she'd always yearned to be on television. "I know I never will," she said. But then she shared a secret with me. She has some media influence even though she's on the viewer's side of the TV screen. She watches a televised church program. She told me: "One evening I was watching as the minister preached a salvation message. He was declaring the power of the blood of Jesus to forgive sins, but he seemed to be having a hard time. Behind him, two choir members slept, lulled by the hot lights. Suddenly it dawned on me that this was a live telecast. I would never be *on* that program, but I could do something *about* it."

She said she dropped to her knees in front of the TV set and began praying for the minister to be strengthened. Then she added, "And, Lord, wake up those two sleeping people who are a bad witness and a distraction to what God is saying through Your servant." She told me, "Betty, the man who had had his head back and mouth open suddenly looked very alert. And the older woman in the second row yawned slightly, put her hand over her mouth with a twinge of embarrassment, and sat up straight for the conclusion of the program."

Not all prayers for other people are answered so quickly. Sometimes answers come because of persevering prayer.

Recently a neurosurgeon in the Dakotas, trained in medical skills in Houston and at the Mayo Clinic, operated on a young mother. His work was so successful that she was back to her full-time work in a week. He was one of the first doctors to use the new laser system of brain surgery. What was his background? Two ordinary farm women who knew him as a lad roaming through the sunflower fields and sliding down haystacks, took it upon themselves to have coffee together and pray for him at 7:00 A.M. every day. His natural gifts and abilities, coupled with his learned skills and knowledge, energized by two women plugged in to the Battery of all power and wisdom, launched that young M.D. What a team!

Over the past eleven years, I have seen some impossible answers to prayer. In the Appendix I include a list of prayer specialists who are in tune with particular needs of people.

They've had a miracle and want to pray for people who have the same need they once had. The prayers of two people are stronger than the prayers of one. I firmly believe that God will give *you* a miracle if He knows that you will pray for others who have the same need that you had before your prayer was answered.

Riding upon the High Places

Take a look at His amazing promise in Isaiah 58:6–14: "Is not this the fast that I have chosen? to loose the bands of wickedness, to undo the heavy burdens, and to let the oppressed go free, and that ye break every yoke? Is it not to deal thy bread to the hungry, and . . . bring the poor . . . to thy house, . . . [cover] the naked, and . . . hide not thyself from thine own flesh? *Then* shall thy light break forth as the morning, and thine health shall spring forth speedily: and thy righteousness shall go before thee; the glory of the Lord shall be thy rearward. Then shalt thou call, and the Lord shall answer . . . Here I am. If thou take away from the midst of thee the yoke . . . and satisfy the afflicted soul; *then* shall thy light rise in obscurity, and thy darkness be as the noon day: and the Lord shall guide thee continually, and satisfy thy soul in drought, and make fat thy bones: and thou shalt be like a watered garden, and like a spring of water, whose waters fail not . . . If thou . . . call the sabbath a delight, the holy of the Lord. . . not doing thine own ways . . . *Then shalt thou delight thyself in the Lord; and I will cause thee to ride upon the high places of the earth* . . . The mouth of the Lord hath spoken it" (italics added).

If you are investing, in tune with God's people, He will take care of your needs.

3

In Tune with
Women

"*Each of you should look not only to your own interests, but also to the interests of others.*"

Philippians 2:4, NIV

Only a woman can understand the needs of another woman.

I never had a sister, just four brothers. My father, Glenn Perkins, is one of the few living saints I know, but he never understood me like Mother. Our female natures drew us together.

Last year I made my first trip across the ocean. For a month I was in South Africa and Zimbabwe. While in Durbin I had an amazing experience that reminded me of the bond women have with each other. After I'd spoken one evening, I autographed books and prayed with many people. The crowd had dwindled but I noticed an attractive young woman with two tiny children, waiting, obviously wanting to speak with me.

When I sat down by her, she whispered, "My life has changed tonight. I asked Jesus to forgive my past and clean me up and give me direction for the future." I rejoiced with her but knew there was something more she wanted to say. "Mrs. Malz," she continued, "it isn't fair. You're a good woman and you wear cheap plastic bracelets." (She was right. They matched my outfit, but they were three tiny, thin bands of ivory colored plastic. I had paid ten cents for them at a garage sale.) She went on, "I wear diamonds, ivory, and gold. I am—or I was until tonight—a well-paid prostitute. I've made love to wealthy diamond miners, gold merchants. Please wear my bracelets."

She slipped her jewelry off her wrist and placed it in my hand. I accepted it, sensing that this gift was a symbol of the turning point in her life.

I hugged her, I wept with her. I brought her bracelets back home with me and when I wear them I pray for the prayer request that was on her heart: "I have no husband," she said, "no father for these two babies. I need a Christian mate, or a new job because I cannot go back to the old even though I'm not trained for anything else."

When I think of this woman I, on one hand, list all the things that make our lives different from the other. We live on separate continents. We live on two different economic planes. We are years apart in age. We've had different circles of friends and acquaintances. We've had different careers, spent our days and nights in environments that could hardly be more foreign to each other.

But compared to all those things that might separate us from each other, we could communicate so deeply, I could personally sense her joy and her sorrow, because we shared the common bond of womanhood.

My friend Joyce Simmons has written a book with a great theme. Shared joy is double the joy, shared sorrow is half the sorrow. Actually this is a very old principle. Romans 12:15 says, "Rejoice with those who rejoice; mourn with those who mourn" (NIV).

Although this is a directive to all Christians I think it is especially important for women to tune in to each other, to strengthen each other's faith, to help each other stay tuned in to God.

When I first started speaking I avoided talking to women's groups. I preferred speaking to mixed groups or simply to a whole church group. But as I prayed I became tuned in to the fact that women have greater needs than men.

There are complex reasons for this. Women today are pulled in a thousand different directions. The television screen, magazines, books, pulpits, classrooms are all full of experts telling them who they should be. And every expert has sure-fire advice that conflicts with the last piece of advice spoken with an equal amount of authority.

But all women do not have the same goals. We are individuals, not clones. Although all women have the same basic desires—for health, to know God, for personal relationships, for creative fulfillment—our needs are varied and complex.

Whereas women in past generations haven't had as much choice about their circumstances, women today have a cafeteria of choices.

Recently, thank God, it is no longer possible to classify woman's work. (I flew 192,000 air miles last year, and on one recent flight, as I deplaned, I poked my nose in the cockpit and said, "That was the smoothest landing I've ever had." "Thank you," a sweet soprano voice replied.

Then another voice, deep bass, chimed in, "Wasn't *she* terrific?")

Women are now making new choices with God's help. This cultural change is great but it can churn up indecision and emotional need in some women who are facing new vistas for the first time.

Many women are frustrated because they grew up too fast and were never able to enjoy the free spirit of childhood innocence, imagination, and uncomplicated joy.

My daughter Brenda has two children. She is aggravated when visitors ask her young daughter, Erika, "Do you have a boyfriend?" as if that were the prime question of life for a girl in elementary school. Our daughters need to learn more from us than how to snag men!

The needs of women that aren't generally shared by men aren't all cultural. As far back as Eve in the garden God acknowledged that sin—rebellion against God—would affect women differently from the way it affects men. To Adam, God said, "By the sweat of your brow you will eat your food" (Genesis 3:19, NIV). To Eve, He said, "I will greatly increase your pains in childbearing. . . . Your desire will be for your husband, and he will rule over you" (3:16). While both men and women would feel physical consequences for their sin, woman—not man—seems to carry a load that is more emotionally centered. One part of a woman is individual, the other part is ever searching for someone to surrender her freedom to. Some use their husbands as this support instead of stretching toward God.

When I realized the needs of my "sisters," I prayed the words of Solomon, "Give thy servant an understanding heart" (1 Kings 3:9). Now, to understand something, you have to stand *under* it.

The Biggest Obstacle

My daughter April plays on her college's women's basketball team. Last week I watched her play. She scored eight points, but the statistics showed that she had ten assists and ten rebounds. I was proud of her "support" approach to winning the game. And in a like manner, if we women are to understand each other— stand under each other or support each other—we must cut the throat of our biggest enemy: jealousy and a competitive spirit.

In high school I learned the deadly power of jealousy. One of my classmates, an intelligent, beautiful girl, ran for the position of class president. Another candidate was a rather homely and dull girl, not nearly as sharp. There were more girls than boys in my class, and the girls voted in the unattractive candidate just so they wouldn't feel threatened by the other's good looks *and* title.

Too often women hold onto a childish pattern: If I can't have a piece of candy, you can't have one either. Have you ever noticed that it's easier to mourn with someone who's mourning than to rejoice with someone else who's received something that you'd very much like to have for yourself?

Wise Solomon—the one who'd asked God for the gift of understanding—was asked to judge a case that involved a jealous woman.

The story goes like this:

Now two prostitutes came to the king and stood before him. One of them said, "My lord, this woman and I live in the same house. I had a baby while she was there with me. The third day after my child was

61

born, this woman also had a baby. We were alone; there was no one in the house but the two of us.

"During the night this woman's son died because she lay on him. So she got up in the middle of the night and took my son from my side while I your servant was asleep. She put him by her breast and put her dead son by my breast. The next morning, I got up to nurse my son—and he was dead! But when I looked at him closely in the morning light, I saw that it wasn't the son I had borne."

The other woman said, "No! The living one is my son; the dead one is yours."

But the first one insisted . . . And so they argued before the king. . . .

Then the king said, "Bring me a sword." So they brought a sword for the king. He then gave an order: "Cut the living child in two and give half to one and half to the other."

The woman whose son was alive was filled with compassion for her son and said to the king, "Please, my lord, give her the living baby! Don't kill him."

But the other said, "Neither I nor you shall have him. Cut him in two!"

Then the king gave his ruling: "Give the living baby to the first woman. Do not kill him; she is his mother."

(1 Kings 3:16–27, NIV)

Doesn't the scenario sound familiar? "If I can't have it, you can't either."

Jealousy is a many-layered emotion, but both it and envy are listed in Galatians 5 as desires that are contrary to the Spirit. Right before that listing of sins, Paul reminds us of the law that "is summed up in a single command: 'Love your neighbor as yourself.' " Then he continues, "If you keep on biting and devouring each other, watch out or you will be destroyed by each other" (5:14–15, NIV).

When I see jealousy creep into the heart of a woman I look deeper for root cause and I often discover a woman who needs to feel accepted for who she is and where she is. She needs to know that she is valued.

When you meet an angry, frustrated woman, pray for her. Tune in to her need, assist her to be what God initially planned for her. I have had the joy of restoring an old 1962 MGA and a hundred-year-old farm house. But how much more joy there is in helping restore depressed, battered, misunderstood, neglected women! David said, "He restoreth my soul." God can restock our shelves through meaningful friendships with other women. I believe God has a very specialized calling for women who will tune in to the needs of other women and seek to meet them with His help.

A Lesson from History

I'm fascinated by stories of pioneer women who kept moving West, opening up the frontier. In history books she's too frequently ignored or stereotyped. But these women were varied and complex individuals, just as women are today.

Whether pioneer women were tough or fragile, whether they entered the frontier by choice or by duty, their letters, diaries and personal accounts reveal a common thread: These women needed each other. Life was difficult and a bond drew them together for comfort, support and understanding.

Unlike their husbands, many women had not abandoned their old homes with a sense of joy and adventure. Their wedding vows ("Whither thou goest, I will go") bound them to pick up roots, but many were heartsick with the move into the great unknown. Many were leaving the comforts of Eastern middle-class life to venture into a lonely life of insecurity and uncertainty. I can't imagine the stress and discomfort of the physical journey—weeks or months of covered wagon living (the original mobile home!). Everything you owned was in that small canvas-covered box.

On the trail, women hardly sat back and enjoyed the bumpy ride. They cooked, cleaned, managed the children, nursed the sick, drove the teams, fed the livestock, and gave birth. They daily faced the realities of possible death: The trail was marked by hundreds of graves.

At the end of the trail conditions improved little. Their supplies were depleted by the long journey and their first harvest was a long way off. One woman wrote that she set up housekeeping with "just one stew kettle . . . three butcher knives . . . just two sheets and one little bit of a bed with a few feathers in it. . . . I cut up the sheets to make shirts for my husband and then we had none."

Death took its heaviest toll among the women and children, though often enough the men did not survive and women were left to face the frontier experience alone. By 1890 statistics indicate that a quarter of a million women—most of them widows—were running their own farms and ranches.

Through all this, women needed and leaned heavily on one another for assistance, compassion, understanding, and companionship. Without each other's support, they didn't survive. One settler in Wisconsin, Augusta Levy, described the women's bond as a source of "courage and pluck." This common bond worked as a springboard for the development of communities and social structure that transformed a lawless region. Women meant families, and families required order—churches, schools, libraries, survival.

"Courage and pluck." That's what women who were bound together by need gave to each other and it's what women today need from each other.

Woman to Woman

One of the best books I've read about a woman being in tune is nearly thirty years old, yet it's still as fresh today as it was then: *Woman to Woman* by Eugenia Price. She starts her chapter on friendships with the following tragic anecdote. A widow, about fifty-five, jumped to her death from her apartment on the twelfth floor. On her desk, she left this note: "I can't stand one more day of this loneliness. No sound from my telephone. No mail in my box. No friends." On the sixth floor of the same building lived another widow. She told reporters: "I wish I had known she was so lonely. I could have called on her. We could have been friends."

Two women, living in the same building, *could* have reached out to each other. But they didn't. I saw another version of this story in my own mailbox. One day I got two letters from the same city. Both writers, two women, were lonely for friendship and someone to go to church with, to drink coffee with. I looked at the return addresses and could hardly believe that one lived at 1503 S. 7th Street and the other at 1522 S. 8th Street. Now this story has a happy ending. I saw the need and an obvious solution:

I mailed each woman the other's letter, and, as a result, they have become fast friends.

The answer to loneliness is reaching out—especially to other women. Later on in the same chapter, Eugenia Price says, "If He (Jesus) is first with us, we *have* to give of ourselves to other people. This requires no premeditation on our part. We may resist inwardly or even outwardly for a minute, but if He is in control, we end up giving! Because He is the great Giver."

I was very interested in a chapel address given by Marilyn Kingsriter. She specifically spoke to the women, commenting, "A young woman student makes a mistake to develop relationships only with men. You really only develop one such lifelong friendship, your mate. But you can have *many* friendships with women that contribute richly for a lifetime."

How true this is, and those women don't necessarily have to be women our own age. In his letter to Titus, Paul says that it is important for the older women to teach the younger women how to be godly women and good wives and mothers (Titus 2:4–5). There are many benefits to being a grandmother, and one of them is having experience, which can be passed on to younger mothers.

When you want to know how to get to Bismarck, North Dakota, you don't ask someone who is planning to go, you find someone who has made a successful trip there.

Teaching the Next Generation

In one seminar a young mother told me, "I feel like a letter someone slipped under my husband's door with no return address. My husband doesn't have friends, just contacts. He is too busy to contact even me. When we go out, I sit at the children's end of the table (the conversational junkyard). I feel I'm running in place like my kid's caged pets. I feel like I'm struggling to remain in a chair that has been pulled out from under me." As I listened, I thought, *This young mother needs an older woman as a friend. She needs someone who can help ease the load of her two young children, so she's not so rigidly caged in, so she has energy to work on her marriage.* My heart reaches out for the brilliant, trained young woman who loves her babies dearly but feels trapped wiping noses and behinds all day.

Be patient during the years you have little ones under your feet. Soon you will be able to assist and equip others who come to you for help.

Being a grandmother myself, I know that a mother is a *teacher* and a *creature* with real human needs. But by nature she'll often sacrifice herself with her children.

A friend of mine in Watertown, South Dakota, is a Methodist minister's wife and teaches the fourth grade. She asked the children in her class to do a special assignment and answer in their own words, What Is a Grandmother? A nine-year-old boy won the essay contest. Laugh with me as you read it.

What Is a Grandmother?

A grandmother is a lady who has no children of her own. She likes other people's little girls and boys. A grandfather is a man grandmother. He goes for walks with the boys, and they talk about fishing and stuff like that.

Grandmothers don't have to do anything except be there. They are old so they shouldn't play hard or run. It is enough if they take us shopping where the pretend horse is, and have a lot of dimes ready. Or if they take us for walks they should slow down past things like pretty leaves and caterpillars. They never say "hurry up" like mothers do.

Usually grandmothers are fat, but not too fat to tie your shoes. They wear glasses and funny underwear. They can take their teeth and gums off.

Grandmothers don't have to be smart, only answer questions like "Why isn't God married?" and "How come dogs chase cats?"

Grandmothers don't talk baby talk like visitors do, because it is too hard to understand. When they read to you they don't skip pages and don't mind reading the same story over and over again.

Everybody should try to have a grandmother, especially if you don't have a television. They are the only grownups who have time.

Right now I am staying in a little fishing village on the Gulf Coast of Florida hiding from people, the television, and the telephone, so I can write this book. There are pelicans nearby and yesterday an old woman told me an interesting story about them.

When the water temperature gets colder than 68 degrees, the Gulf fish swim down too deep for the pelicans to pluck them out of the water. If this happens and a mother pelican can't get fish for her babies, she will, as a last resort, cut into her own breast with her beak and nurse her baby with her blood.

In a national magazine I read about a group of Boy Scouts that was camping in the mountains when their van overturned. All but one boy were rescued and he was clinging precariously to a tree limb between two rocks on a precipice. The forest rangers and a fire patrol had tried to reach him. Then onlookers watched as a woman was hoisted up the incline. One news reporter remarked, "She'll reach him, she's his mother!" She did.

I have a relative who teaches elementary-school math. She asked one little girl, "How many children in your family?" The girl replied, "Three."

"How many parents?"

"Two."

"Then," the teacher asked, "if you divide pie into equal parts for your family, how many pieces would you serve?"

The girl said, "Four."

The teacher corrected, "But you have five members in your family."

The child had it all figured out, "You don't know my mommie. She would say she didn't want any so we could have a bigger piece."

I laughed at the story—because it sounded so familiar. Some things never change, and motherhood is one of them.

In the *New York Times* I recently read that the "eighties" woman is really very much like her grandmother. "Although her path into family life and the work world may seem to be blazing new trails, she is not a pioneer, but is returning to old ground for new reasons."

Solomon offered the same message: "There is nothing new under the sun." God merely renews it and reviews it to each generation through a simple, trusting, praying woman.

History doesn't repeat itself, but women can help repeat the good of history. The in-tune woman is aware of the past as she looks to the future. We understand life backward, but it must be lived forward. I have no desire to go back to using an ice pick, and wait for an ice man to deliver a fifty-pound cake of ice, that has melted to forty pounds by the time he gets to my old-fashioned ice box. I enjoy my refrigerator with its automatic defrost and icemaker; and yet, something is lost with convenience.

Although we can and should enjoy modern conveniences and be willing to throw out what no longer fits (clean out the closets!), some things from the past should be kept and passed down. Many women with tunnel vision are missing a lot by not listening, learning from older women. One woman told me with a sigh, "If only I could relate to the women I'm related to." Some search far, when great knowledge is near.

My Aunt Gwen helps keep me in touch with my family's traditions. She helps merge my past with the present. She helps remind me of the traditions I want to pass on to my children and grandchildren. Each fall my grandparents served pumpkin seed tea, and every spring we ate fresh, wild dandelion greens cooked with a few drops of apple cider vinegar. (It was our "spring tonic.") My son-in-law indulges me with a smile while I pass down those family traditions and others—like eating cabbage on New Year's Day so you will have greenbacks in your wallet all year—to his children Erika and Ryan.

What else has the older generation taught me that I've passed on to my daughters? The importance of family devotions and prayer each night. Even if overnight guests were visiting, my grandparents asked everyone present in their home at bedtime to kneel for prayer together. It has been a stabilizing influence in my life. Don't change what works. What a strong cloth of "will be" can be woven from two threads: "is" and "was." If godly women would take time to teach the younger women, to pass on the torch of prayer, we can become flame women, lighthouse ladies. The hard-learned insight of an older woman, coupled with the anticipation of a younger woman, is a winning combination that produces future success.

Do you remember the biblical story of Ruth and Naomi? Now there was a winning combination. Naomi's long life had been hard on her. To escape famine, she and her husband and two sons had fled their hometown of Bethlehem and settled in the country of Moab. But her husband died there, as did her two sons who had taken young brides of their own.

Eventually, when Naomi heard that there was food back in Bethlehem, she got ready to return home. But she didn't travel alone. Ruth, her daughter-in-law, had grown very attached to Naomi and insisted that she would leave her homeland of Moab and stay with Naomi for the rest of her life.

When Ruth and Naomi had settled into Bethlehem, Naomi gave Ruth some invaluable advice on how to go about finding a Hebrew husband. She should make her presence more obvious to Boaz, a landowner and near kinsman. Now Ruth could have discounted the advice but, rather, she weighed it and saw the value of it. She went to Boaz. And how did he respond? He said, "This kindness is greater than that which you showed earlier: You have not run after the younger men, whether rich or poor. And now, my daughter, don't be afraid. I will do for you all you ask" (Ruth 3:10–11, NIV) . . . which is to say that they married. (And had a son who was the grandfather of King David.)

You may be thinking, Well, that might work fine for Ruth but you don't know my mother-in-law. . . . And you're absolutely right; every life situation is different. God may not have set a wise woman friend in your path, but if you reach out in friendship to other women of all ages, if you give of yourself, others will give back to you.

Did Ruth receive the benefit of Naomi's life-changing advice while their relationship was brand-new? No. It came after Ruth had gone way out of her way to show her love and faithfulness to Naomi.

That's what friendship is all about—reaching out. As Proverbs 18:24 says, "A man that hath friends must shew himself friendly."

I know an older woman who is a retired missionary. Does she wait for God to bring other women to her doorstep? Hardly. Weekly she writes three young missionary wives in three different countries. She encourages them, sends them clippings that might help inspire them or that they could use in their teaching; she prays for them daily. She's in tune with women. She broadens her influence. She becomes a cosmopolitan woman.

Women in Service

What are we to set our energies behind?

There's no formula answer to that question; we have a Father who asks that we dial direct! He wants each person to dig out His will from His Word.

In his Pentecost sermon, Peter quoted an Old Testament passage, Joel 2:28–32, that makes it clear that God's Spirit is given to women and that He intends to use women to spread His word. The Lord said to Joel, "I will pour out my Spirit on all people. . . . On my servants, both men and women, I will pour out my Spirit in those days, and they will prophesy" (Acts 2:17–18, NIV).

In God's Kingdom there is no such thing as second-class citizenship for women. I don't believe that when God passes out talent and gifts, He even looks at the sex organs of a human being. The Bible tells us that Lydia was a Christian business-woman. She had a shop in Thyatira and dealt in purple fabrics.

Jill Briscoe feels that if the church would discard its tunnel vision where the female is concerned, more women would concentrate on the work of the church for satisfaction and creative fulfillment instead of leaving home to satisfy this need inside them. One woman told Mrs. Briscoe, "I hate pouring Kool-Aid and teaching kindergarten, but it's all the church allows me to do. I honestly have more pleasure with unchurched people. They let me develop."

Jesus encouraged women to develop themselves. Repeatedly He treated women with a respect that far surpassed the culture He lived in. In public He called a woman a "daughter of Abraham" (Luke 13:16) when sons only were recognized in such an honorable way. He forthrightly told the Samaritan woman that He was the Messiah and she, in turn, evangelized her whole town. On Easter morning, He first appeared to women who then told the disciples of His resurrection.

Now God has called me to be a writer. I am not a woman minister—and I have no desire to be one. But as I stay tuned to God's voice, He tells me to share His message. And I must obey His voice just as women did in Bible times:

Micah 6:4 and Exodus 15:20 refer to Miriam as a leader of the wandering children of Israel.

Deborah was the chief ruler of Israel for forty years, giving orders to the army's generals (Judges 4–5).

The prophetess Huldah spoke the word of the Lord to an all-male delegation, including priest Hilkiah. Revival was kindled throughout the nation when her word was heeded (2 Kings 22).

Anna prophesied in the Temple, declaring that Mary's son was the Messiah (Luke 2).

Philip's four daughters were evangelists, like their father (Acts 21:8–9).

Euodias and Syntyche were women and leaders in the church at Philippi (Philippians 4:2–3).

Deaconess Phoebe and Priscilla are the first in a long list of men and women Paul salutes at the Roman church (Romans 16).

The women of Corinth publicly prayed and prophesied (1 Corinthians 11:4–5).

One of Jo Berry's books is titled *The Priscilla Principle* and there she presents a summary statement that is based on her study of this influential New Testament woman's life. Jo recommends "The Priscilla Principle" as a basis for every woman's life: "Every facet of each Christian woman's life must be looked upon as an ongoing ministry, dedicated to the Lord Jesus Christ. What she does should be determined by the leading of the Holy Spirit, her giftedness, and the opportunities for service that God sets in her paths. She must take personal responsibility for defining God's will and developing a theology of ministry based on a thorough knowledge of the Scriptures."

I believe that if a woman is exercising her God-given talent winsomely and graciously, she is no threat to the pastor or her husband.

On a visit to a church in Edmonton, Alberta, I was delighted to see my young friend Erica Riehl competently carrying on her husband's pastoral work. He had suffered a heart attack and been hospitalized for eight weeks and she capably stepped in.

Johanna Wheeler, a quiet-spoken, interesting young woman, is serving as associate pastor at Central Assembly in Springfield, Missouri. The pastor there, Phil Wannenmacher, has wisely rounded out his staff and faculty by tuning in to modern contemporary needs. There are many avenues of creativity that women can develop. Who has better understanding to counsel on subjects like childbearing, menopause, P.M.S., or pregnancy than another woman?

No two women are talented or called in exactly the same way. No two women are placed in the same circumstances or given the same opportunities. But I can assure every woman of one thing: There's enough need to go around. God wants to meet those needs and some He's earmarked for you. Tune in and He'll lead you to a need you can meet.

4

In Tune with Men

"*Submit to one another out of reverence for Christ.*"

Ephesians 5:21, NIV

Long before a woman marries that desire surges to give herself completely to someone, to have a deep soul relationship with another, to be loved thoroughly and exclusively. The desire to pair off and settle down has been part of a woman's life for centuries.

When I was in first grade our teacher Zora Kern went around the room and asked each student, "What do you want to be when you grow up?"

Most of the girls replied, "Nurse." Most of the boys said, "Fireman" or "Policeman." But I said, "When I grow up, I want to be a mother." The kids laughed at me.

Of course at that age any thought of being a mother was based on the assumption that I'd first be a wife—in tune with one special man. But I had no idea how important it was to be in tune with God *before* that special day when I'd walk down the aisle and say, "I do."

Until Then

I think God looks down on young women and older women and speaks His perfect will, words to this effect:

"I love you, My child, and until you discover that only in Me is your satisfaction to be found, you will not be capable of the perfect human relationship that I have planned for you. I want you to stop planning, stop wishing, and allow Me to give you the most thrilling plan existing—one that you can't imagine. I want you to have the *best*. Please allow Me to bring it to you. Just keep watching Me, expecting the greatest things. Keep experiencing that satisfaction of knowing that I am. Keep learning and listening to the things I tell you. . . .

"Don't be anxious. Don't worry. Don't look around at the things others have gotten or that I've given them. Don't look at the things you think you want. You just keep looking at Me, or you'll miss what I want to show you.

"And then, when you're ready, I'll surprise you with a love far more wonderful than any would ever dream. You see, until you are ready, and until the one I have for you is ready (I am working even now to have both of you ready at the same time), until you are both satisfied exclusively with Me and the Life I have prepared for you, you won't be able to experience the Love that exemplifies your relationship with Me.

"And, dear one, I want you to have this most wonderful Love. I want you to see in the flesh a picture of your relationship with Me, and to enjoy materially and concretely the everlasting union of beauty and perfection and Love that I offer you with Myself. Know that I love you utterly. I am God Almighty. Believe and be satisfied."

I believe if we would teach our daughters that loving God, finding the *right* mate, or doing something worthwhile until he comes along is more important than snagging a husband early, we could change the statistics: After tonsillectomy, abortion is now the second most frequently performed operation in our country.

Age doesn't necessarily have anything to do with desperation. I've seen widows get so preoccupied looking for new husbands that they jeopardize the happiness of their former in-laws, neglect their children, and separate themselves from close friends who could have helped them bridge the gap of change. They obviously were not sure of who they were in their own right without men at their sides. As girls, too many women were (and still are) bootlegged into thinking that you are who you marry and who you mother. No woman is successful if she does not support her man, develop her offspring. But sometimes this is a foreclosure of identity. It may not be possible to piggyback oneself to satisfaction.

After the Yoking Ceremony

As I've mentioned, my car is an old 1962 MGA convertible. It is dark British-racing green and has wonderful spoke wheels. I keep it because it still gets such good mileage—37 miles to the gallon. It's doing better now than it once did. When we moved to North Dakota, I began having engine trouble. I wondered if this would be the end of the line for it. But fortunately, a student at Trinity College had worked on foreign cars when he'd been in the military. It didn't take him long to diagnose the problem. "Your carbs are out of synch," he said. And once he'd synchronized the dual carburetors, it hummed again.

Marriage is like this. If one of the team is out of synch, or out of tune, with the other, there's trouble. To use another image, if one tire is "puffed up" (prideful and self-centered) the ride is bumpy for everyone in the car.

One quarrel with my husband cost me eleven barren writing days on this book. I couldn't sleep peacefully and soundly at night; I lost the free spirit I need to create and write during the daytime. Now I can't afford to waste that kind of time. I need to stay in tune with my spouse.

How does marriage work? Joy is at the start of it. Sharing is a part of it. And love is the heart of it. But every marriage license should read, "Note: Some assembly required."

Marriage is not intramural competition, but a blend of individuality and mutuality. A married couple should be like a pair of matching bookends—not glued together, but holding up separate ends of a family unit; partners for a purpose. They also could be compared to salt and pepper shakers, both necessary for a well-set table but holding separate ingredients. Or think of two logs: To burn properly they cannot be jammed together. They must be close together, but yet there must be enough space between for oxygen to pass through. To flame properly they must have room to breathe. Despite what some people say, it is possible to "belong" to someone without being attached like a tandem. I like to see a couple yoked together as a side-by-side team. I feel sorry for the human being who always has to follow shadow with only a "rear" view—like the second or third rank in an Alaskan dogsled team. No tailgating allowed. To paraphrase a bumper sticker I saw recently, if you're not the lead dog, the scenery never changes.

While I'm here in Florida, friends occasionally send me tapes of my husband's chapel messages. I just received one on which he spoke to men only. I liked what he said:

"It takes a certain kind of meanness for an inferior guy to hit a superior gal with Ephesians five and yell, 'Submit!' If she's better than you are, then grow into it. Marriage should evolve into the mutual love of watching each other live.

"Marriage is not a safety net for men. Some men take the warrior-aristocrat stance, as if their wives were peasants, 'Give me what I want and I will protect you against me.' But a wife is not a man's year-round fireplace. I've seen married bums lie on couches and drink beer, burping, scratching in their sweaty undershirts, mumbling commands. Some unmotivated men marry a woman's vitality so her batteries will be theirs. Like all-purpose enriched flour, they want an all-purpose wife."

Carl informed those young men that society is changing, and he wanted them to be like good railroad flagmen and brakemen. They know that if you want to jump from a moving train (without getting injured or killed), you jump with, not against, the forward motion.

A lot of men who suffer inflated personal egos say—by words or actions—"Don't become informed, don't learn too much, because I want to continue to manipulate you into satisfying my needs." But the wise man will nurture his wife to become her best person. In turn, a wise woman will support, submit to, and give herself to that loving relationship of being equally yoked.

It is possible to become a powerful team, partners for a purpose, but it is necessary always to submit to *each other* in love as you both—separately and collectively—submit to God.

The often-quoted "Wives, submit to your husbands" (Ephesians 5:22, NIV) is immediately preceded by a less familiar verse: "Submit to one another out of reverence for Christ."

A good capable driver would never think of turning over the keys of her new car to an inexperienced driver who had no license just because he was a male, yet women will turn over the running of a home, family, and more important matters to a less-than-capable man—just because a seminar lecturer tells her that men should be in charge. (Read 1 Samuel 25 and Acts 5:1–11 to discover two stories that show that a wife isn't expected to abdicate all responsibility when she marries.) Some men who conduct these seminars aren't brave enough to get married themselves, yet they are quick to give advice about it. Pardon my saying so, but if I have to listen to one more tape or one more lecture by an unmarried man roaring "Submit!" and eat humble pie while he dines on pecan pie a la mode, I think I shall choke.

Don't misunderstand me. Anything with two heads is a monster. Bossy, domineering women who must "run the show" are obnoxious. (So are bossy, domineering men.) Yet, by contrast, women who only express their view of their husband's dreams are in trouble.

God's idea of a good marriage isn't based on a stifled personality. Throughout the New Testament God continually asks His people to encourage one another, to help one another use their talents and gifts to the full benefit of the Kingdom.

I have a talented friend who is married to a high-achiever. She says the right supportive things, gives her husband affirming glances, but her parents and family members notice that she keeps gaining weight, that she seems more and more nervous, that her complexion has gone from good to bad to worse. She is known among acquaintances as a "throne polisher"— his. She seems like a balloon pushed under the water. On one level she seems to be under control, but her stifled emotions are surfacing in the physical realm.

81

What can a marriage be like?

Recently I attended a Jesse Dixon concert. I particularly enjoyed two of his songs, "Radiate" and "Destined to Win." His songs were Jesus songs and the Holy Spirit helped him sing, but I noticed that his accompanist was always in tune with his songs, his mood. She definitely had the ministry of "helps" and was vitally important to his ability to perform so beautifully. With God's help and the absence of self-centeredness a marriage of two cooperative bound individuals can be like this, although the husband and wife can alternate taking the solo role.

On one visit with Brenda, my heart was warmed when her husband, Bud, put an arm around her and said to me, "Mother, Brenda sacrificed to help me achieve my goal, my doctorate. Now, I want to help some of her dreams come true." Brenda has a degree in music, and Bud has helped her develop a music studio in their home. While she teaches from 5:00 to 8:00 P.M. each evening, he serves dinner to the two children. He bathes them, reads to them, takes them skating, or plays outdoors with them. When she is finished with teaching, they have about a half hour of family time before the children are tucked into bed after prayer. Bud also plays with the children a while on Saturdays so Brenda can have some free time to write.

What a wise man!

When we lived near Houston, Texas, I was amazed at the women from India who came to the University of Medicine. Eight to ten would live in a small apartment, paying a great price to get a medical degree. The minds of many deprived women contain inventions, solutions, and world knowledge locked up inside them. Thank God for a man who recognizes his spouse's potential. Let me add, forgive your husband for not being *everything* you need. Only Jesus is this source.

No Easy Formulas

My first husband, John, owned his own business and followed a consistent schedule. Every day I served all three meals within ten minutes of the same time. Every evening, I had a candle lit and we sat down to eat at 5:00 P.M. Although we enjoyed entertaining and had lots of company, our lives were uncomplicated; we did everything together.

But my second marriage was entirely different. Carl's obligations were many and varied. He was traveling a great deal. Being with people all day, he didn't enjoy entertaining. Sometimes to finish a conversation that was interrupted by the phone or a knock on the door, I had to write him a note or a letter and mail it to the college.

What an adjustment! Life became a continual process of fine-tuning myself to the new situation. At one point, I felt he expected too much. I almost gave up. But I realized my schedule was hard for him, too. We both were having to tolerate, accept, and adjust—to stay in tune. There seem to be three stages in each relationship: emotion, commotion, then devotion. Most lasting marriages grow in love as the couple stays in tune with God and with each other's changing needs.

Ours is not the average marriage. We have quit fretting about this. After being married several years we realized we wanted to step out of the trap of expectations we'd been boxed into: *We* expected our second marriages to be similar to our first, and *other people* kept telling us what they expected our marriage to be. Ours was not the generic union.

We will just make ourselves miserable by trying to please others. But when we relax and put aside unreal expectations we decide we really like what we are and have. When we wake up to the fact that no two marriages are the same—because no two individuals are the same—we can throw off the confining formulas that we can't follow anyway.

After my first book was published, Carl and I both recognized that we had two different ministries, two leadership roles. We agreed that we simply could not attend everything together. Be elastic. Work at being intimate; the sex will follow. One medical doctor explained that sex begins between the ears. "Think tender. Think courtesy. Think intimacy."

We have long hours together in the summer when college is closed, during Christmas break, and spring break. Many times we ride a bike or walk together for as many as six hours—talking, sharing, praying. We enjoy our sexual bond—maybe not at 10:00 P.M. with candlelight, but when we can. Flexibility is essential to survival when both partners are very busy and creative.

Carl has never been able to sleep past 4:00 A.M. He used to work in a bakery. I have tried to get up with him at 4:00 A.M.; he has tried to enjoy everything I do. But when we've done that both of us have been miserable.

Carl and I tried to travel together. He got up at 4:00 A.M. and turned on the lights to read. (He couldn't retreat to another room.) I couldn't sleep. He felt guilty, turned off the light and walked the streets. Then I felt guilty and couldn't sleep anyway. The solution? Now we travel separately most of the time. We are comfortable being like two rails of a train track—side by side, cooperating, without overlapping.

Since I lived alone with two small daughters for six years before I met Carl, I enjoy speaking at singles' retreats. Just before I was leaving to attend a recent retreat, my phone rang and the voice on the other end inquired, "I see in the paper that you are doing a singles' retreat. Is it true that you and Carl are separated?" I could tell that the caller could hardly wait to get some juicy gossip to pass on.

I accommodated and answered, "Yes."

"How long have you been separated?"

"Nine weeks," I replied. I paused (naughty, I know), then added, "He has been on a foreign missions tour, doing retreats for long-term missionary families, and counseling for over two months now."

"Oh, I see," she sighed. I could tell she was disappointed that she had no news to tell.

This winter, I have been in Florida for three months writing. But my physical separation from Carl doesn't indicate any breakdown in our yoked commitment and solid sense of partnership and unity.

Carl and I have been married three wonderful years— sixteen altogether! Looking back, we laugh at those hard adjustments. My first husband, John, and Carl's first wife, Wanda, are probably sitting with their feet propped up on the balcony of heaven, looking down on us, saying, "Poor babies." And then laughingly, "They deserve each other." If we can make it, anyone with God's help can make it!

This morning in the mail I received a homemade Valentine from Carl. In a humorous way he expressed his love.

> Ah, sweet misery of life, at last I've found you.
> You sometimes give me indigestion, but, I'll keep you
> . . . for you, at your worst, are better than most
> women at their very best.

> Love, Carl

Nice, huh?

Avoid women who tell you they fully understand their husbands. They are not sane. (They probably lie about their bowling scores, too.) Don't try to understand everything about your man, you never will. Men are remarkable creatures. I don't understand how airplanes fly, but I travel in them. I don't comprehend electricity, but I enjoy it. And that's the way it is with my husband too. . . .

The Golden Rule

If you have an understanding mate, cherish him. I love what George Eliot wrote: "Oh, the comfort, the inexpressible comfort of feeling safe with a person; having neither to weigh thoughts nor measure words, but to pour them all out, just as they are, chaff and grain together, knowing that a faithful hand will take and sift them, keep what is worth keeping, and then, with the breath of kindness, blow the rest away."

A friend is one with whom you can be your own true self. We should treat and talk to our mates the way we would talk to friends. We would never speak harshly to a friend, a business associate, a church member or employer; why crucify a mate with the tongue? Pairs should fight the devil, not each other.

When Jill Briscoe spoke at Wheaton College, a student asked her, "What is the most important thing in life?"

Jill replied quickly, "The ability to get along with people." That's true of life in general, but especially true in a marriage. Every wife has the power and influential ability to put wings—or buckets of cement—on her husband's feet. As Proverbs 11:29 says, "He that troubleth his own house shall inherit the wind."

I have known men and women who have a "D-Con" personality. D-Con is 99 percent edible corn. But it also contains one percent deadly poison that will kill mice and rats. As Jeremiah 9:8 says, "Their tongue is as an arrow shot out." It is unruly, evil, and full of deadly poison. And James 1:26 says that an unbridled tongue makes a person's religion worthless. It may be a small part of the human body but it is as powerful as a rudder is on a large ship (see James 3).

I recall a little pink card Mother used to have. It read: *"Exhort* = the language of encouragement." There was another that read "Criticism Cripples!"

Carl has counseled family and marriage problems for eighteen years. I have done women's and couples' retreats for eleven years. We've heard and seen heartbreaking story after heartbreaking story. After one of our sessions, a well-manicured couple took us to dinner on the way to the airport. I could hardly believe what I heard. She sounded like a phonograph record—stuck in one groove. Her husband could do nothing right. Everything he said was wrong. If she'd talk to him like this in public, I wondered what she was like in private.

The husband looked as though he wanted to crawl under the table. But then he slipped an arm around her and defended her, "She's been depressed like this since the death of our daughter."

From my point of view there was *no* excuse for her cruelty. I wished I had had some time alone with her so I could get to the bottom of her problem, because I've learned that a critical spirit is often a symptom of deeper discord. (Some couples seem to have been married by the Secretary of War, instead of the Justice of the Peace.) I met one "religious" woman who enjoyed making her unsaved husband jealous of another man: Jesus. To me this is the lowest—and most sacrilegious— form of cruelty.

I've learned that there are three sides to every story: his side, her side, and the truth. Too often selfish concerns distort the truth that could lead to peace. Have you ever noticed that the words *unite* and *untie* contain the same letters? The position of the *I* makes all the difference. Some wives have headaches because their halos are too tight; saints are hard to live with, and husbands feel threatened by this superior, Pharisaical attitude. Many a marriage has been destroyed by self-protection, lack of communication (or too much of it), and an overly sensitive nature.

Parents need to be very careful how they treat their mates. Children learn what kind of wife and husband to be by observation. We have friends who thought it was cute when their daughter "hen-pecked" her husband. But, when their son married a spicy little gal who tried to hen-peck their son, they were very angry. We must remember to apply the Golden Rule (do unto others as you would have them do unto you) and remember the law of the harvest: whatsoever a man soweth, that shall he also reap. Someday a woman will treat your son the way you treated his father.

A Physical Union

I always smile when I think of the Garden of Eden scene: Adam being alone and needing a complementing companion. Even being alone with God was not enough; he needed woman. God then created Eve from Adam's rib and Adam smiled because this woman, "bone of my bones and flesh of my flesh" (Genesis 2:23, NIV), was at his side, knowable and lovable.

In this Genesis account, "becoming one flesh" is mentioned in chapter 2, before the Fall (chapter 3), and I think that the sexual act had central place in that beautiful paradise. It was all we can possibly imagine it to be—union perfected.

With the entrance of sin into the world, reality changed. But I want to propose that God still intends that physical union to be an honorable and mutually pleasurable bond.

Our neighbor recently attended a lecture in downtown St. Petersburg, Florida. The doctor opened the lecture on infertility by commenting on the futility of trying to be what you're not: "Most doctors are men and lie to each other about sex after sixty. If you are in your twenties try daily. If you are in your thirties, try weekly, in the forties, try foreplay, in the fifties try oysters, in the sixties, try anything. Don't compete in the youth arena; get attention by being somebody in your own right." Enjoy your age.

A gynecologist friend suggested that I include a list of foods that stimulate the sex organs. Oysters have a reputation for this, but they're not alone. Try the following: meat, turnips, peppermint, venison, crayfish soup, ginger, lots of water, Chinese food, pepper, eggs, Japanese food, bromide phosphorus, celery, artichokes, calves' brains, milk, asparagus, drug (yohimbin), rice, okra, beets, truffles, carrots, saffron, lots of grapes, and cinnamon.

He also mentioned substances that should be avoided in excess: coffee, tea, lemon, alcohol, soft drinks, and tobacco.

No matter what you eat, aging or poor health (such as anemia or an accident) can hinder the love life in the sex department. But that doesn't indicate a marriage's demise. Smart couples will build on common interests, God's work and ministry to others, friendship, and the wonderful bond of communication. The personality, sense of humor, and spirit of a person can grow and continue to fuel a relationship as long as life remains.

I want to emphasize the beauty of the sex act—as ordained by God. It has a healing, soothing, bonding effect. But in counseling session after counseling session I encounter women who are desperately unhappy in their marriages. And too often, when we cut through the surface problems, I discover the root problem: They feel degraded because their husbands demand oral sexual stimulation.

This was the case—though I did not know it at first—when the wife of a prominent minister once called me out of desperation and unloaded her unhappiness. She had kept her suffering to herself, but, she said, she had been physically and emotionally ill for the three years they had been married. She'd married what she called a "street angel but a house devil." He always made sure that people noticed his courtesy and manners in public, but he was a different person in private.

She said, "I could stand the condescension, if he would not talk so wickedly. In public he shoots velvet arrows, in private he rips me apart with his mouth." I thought of the Scripture in Galatians 5:14–21. "The acts of the sinful nature are obvious. . . Those who live like this will not inherit the kingdom of God" (verses 19, 21, NIV).

I listened for over an hour while this wife poured out her grief and hurt. I had seen her on so many occasions with that "wounded dove" look in her eyes (the Bible says the eyes are the windows of the soul), but I hadn't been able to identify her pain.

At first I suggested that the woman try bragging on her husband like his fans to help control his verbal abuse. Sweet words are very powerful weapons.

She had an answer. "I want to . . . I would love to . . . but he is full of self-centeredness, self-protection, distrust. He always has his guard up. And he's always bragging on himself, telling me how lucky I am to have him. I long to value him and tell him so, but he sings his own praise so loud and long, he squelches me." Then a new series of complaints started.

Before I hung up the phone, I assured her that two of my friends and I would pray for them. Then I suggested that she do what the virgin Mary did. When Joseph, having misunderstood her pregnancy, was ready to "quit" Mary, she zipped her lip, prayed, and waited for God to help her.

Then, several weeks later, I learned the root source of this couple's conflict. The husband demanded that she satisfy him with oral sex.

Now this act is not an expression of love between mates. God ordained sexual love-making for the prime purpose of reproduction, and there are no reproductive organs in the mouth. God made the sex act honorable and pleasurable. When a man and woman have the proper relationship, natural sex leaves a man satisfied as an honored king, a woman as a cherished queen. Oral sex, on the other hand, is a tendency borrowed from the homosexual lifestyle. A man who demands this from a wife is merely degrading another person with his insatiable lust.

Pat Robertson, Jimmy Swaggart, and many others have spoken and written boldly and frankly on this subject. They call it sin, an unclean and unnatural use of the body, as described in Romans 1.

I have no easy answers for women in this situation. Bruising of one's spirit brings a personality bondage. But I stand on the authority of the Word: Jesus came "to set at liberty them that are bruised" (Luke 4:18). There is power in prayer.

Prayer: An Essential Ingredient

If you're convinced that your husband is the big problem point of your marriage, I have one suggestion: Pray about it. Here are ten commandments for a happy marriage:

1. Take care of your own health and appearance.
2. Pray a lot.
3. Develop friendships with other interesting people.
4. Watch and pray.
5. Retain a sense of humor. Increase the mirth rate!
6. Pray fervently.
7. Simplify your life.
8. Pray in faith.
9. Keep your arms open and your mouth shut.
10. Pray without ceasing.

I say, Pray, Pray, Pray. But be prepared to expect most any answer.

One friend of mine, a divorced professional woman, was praying for her ex-husband one morning when the Lord gave her several messages: one for herself, one for her husband, and another for the two collectively. When she wrote them down and reread them, she was shocked to realize that she had been praying that he would return to her so she could make him miserable again. God was asking her to change her attitude. In time, God altered them both and brought them back together in harmony.

Another couple, Ron and Vena Poole, were divorced for eighteen years. As Vena prayed, "Lord teach me how to pray for Ron," the Lord told her to pray for the return of his soul, not his body. She prayed for him every day—not for his return, but that God would overhaul him, restore him. She prayed God's will in her husband's life and for his return to "the fold," the church.

Her obedience paid off. Last January, they were remarried—to each other. They are investing in people now, partners for a purpose, loving and counseling divorced couples—and successfully.

Women don't need to be in such dire circumstances— divorce—before they pray for themselves and their mates.

Once I expressed my "sympathies" to my friend Connie Lundstrom. I hate to travel and I said, "You must love God more than I do to live in a bus for twenty-six years with a husband and four children, traveling three hundred days each year, singing each night, dressing up, smiling."

She grinned, "Don't feel sorry for me. I'd be bored with any other life. Happiness is not doing what I like, but liking what I do. Lowell *is* too busy with everyone else, but I would rather have ten percent of a hundred percent man, than to be forced to have a hundred percent of only a ten percent man. I pray a lot." (Many women complain to me that their husbands are too busy. Perhaps their husbands don't have too much to do, but *they* have too little. Women make allowances if their husbands drink a lot, but won't tolerate a husband who has to work a lot.)

At a women's retreat recently, Karen Schmidgall and I laughed, exchanging woes. Her husband has put his energies into a thriving church in Naperville, Illinois. She says he always has one foot out the door, is always looking for one more mountain to climb. She has learned to enjoy the time they *do* have together. She had a refreshing outlook. She summarized her life by saying, "I'm learning. I'm counseling. I'm praying. I'm becoming an authority on almost every subject but birth control."

We concluded that every woman needs prayer—especially those married to busy men.

A smart woman knows she cannot cope with life. She must have God, be in tune with the Almighty, to help her be in tune with her man. If you are in tune with God, honest and surrendered completely, He will make glorious creative use of your hours and days and relationships—even your blunders. Sometimes stress on a marriage is self-inflicted when mates focus on their inept attempts at perfection while comparing themselves to an imagined ideal that God did not intend any person to reach this side of heaven. God knows we fail. But God wants us to give our special man the best we've got.

5

In Tune with Yourself

"The effect of righteousness will be quietness and confidence forever."

Isaiah 32:17, NIV

No matter where you go . . . there you are! No matter where *I* go, there I am. You can't escape yourself; you might as well face yourself. You never go so far but what your tail (or tale) follows you. Think about the following story for a moment.

Her mother was a famous beauty. She was an ugly duckling. The relatives didn't hesitate to say it. When visitors called the young girl would hide and suck her fingers till her mother called after her, "Come in, Granny." The mother would then explain to guests, "She's such a funny child, so old-fashioned, we call her Granny."

Her mother died when the girl was eight; her father, an alcoholic, died when she was nine. She was shipped off to live with her grandmother, a strict disciplinarian. At fifteen the girl had no friends her own age, and at eighteen she was presented to society—which shuddered at what they saw and heard: the girl was six feet tall, had a scratchy, loud voice; her front teeth protruded; she would giggle at odd times; and she wouldn't wear cosmetics. Occasionally she would burst into tears. The family thought she was "out of tune."

But there is life after puberty. One of her cousins proposed marriage to her and, despite his mother's three years of protest, the couple married March 17, 1905. Since her dad was dead, Uncle Teddy gave her away. She had one thing going for her: She had inherited her uncle's energy. "Not proper in a woman," everyone clucked.

In 1913 when her husband was stricken with polio, his mother demanded that he hide from public life, retire to her own home. But his doctor and wife encouraged him to return to politics from his wheelchair. When he did, his mother remarked, "I'm getting weaker in my son's life. His wife is getting stronger. She's in the lead." Although his wife was his eyes and ears, she didn't find a place in his arms. He fell in love with his young secretary, Lucy, and forced his wife to open her arms to the poor.

Her husband was elected governor, then President of the U.S. At the inaugural, he arranged a front-row seat and private limousine for his lover, the lovely Lucy. But the First Lady held her head up and became her husband's legs. She covered forty thousand miles every year for him, delivered lectures, visited slums, nursery schools, playgrounds, and sharecroppers. While the wife was away, Lucy called on and sometimes stayed with the President. Once he had the presidential train sidetracked in New Jersey so he could visit her estate. Undaunted, the First Lady held a press conference once a week and wrote a question and answer page for *Woman's Home Companion*. Her own column "My Day" appeared in 135 newspapers. Her twice-weekly broadcasts were sponsored by Sweetheart soap, Simmons Mattress, Johns-Manville Building Supply, Selby Shoes, and Pond's Cold Cream, and she gave all proceeds to the American Friends Service Committee. On one occasion she kept two White House receptions going at once, moving back and forth through the connecting door.

The President continued to meet Lucy. Cartoonists continued to poke fun at the First Lady's face. Yet she kept right on working, successfully debating Winston Churchill and Joseph P. Kennedy. She was still doing her husband's work when he died, with Lucy by his side. She wept only briefly, then steadied *herself*.

Wounded by her mother, father, mother-in-law, her husband, she now embraced all humanity, continued her column, wrote fifteen books, reformed Tammany Hall, and represented the United States at the United Nations. Year after year American women voted her the woman they most admired. The Gallup Poll reported her, "Most popular woman in any part of the world." She replied, "Back of tranquillity lies, always, conquered unhappiness."

At age seventy-four she wrote: "We must regain a vision of *ourselves* as leaders of the world, America, join in an effort to use all knowledge for the good of all human beings. When we do that, we shall have nothing to fear." When she died her headstone bore the words, "The only thing we have to fear is fear itself."

She was in tune with herself. She was Eleanor Roosevelt.

The Real Villain

I included this story of Eleanor Roosevelt to show you how important it is to be secure in who you are—in tune with yourself no matter how chaotic the world around you may be.

In this chapter I want to help you see how you "fine-tune" yourself. This was the need one well-known woman confided in me: "I fasted and prayed that God would use me. In quiet reflection I learned the origin of my deadlock. It was not the wrong major or the wrong mate. Deep down I knew it. When all other false scapegoats had been exhausted, I began to creep up on the real villain: myself. I was not steady, I was divided against myself." That day she determined to pray until, with God's help, she found the place where she was in tune with herself. That same day, as she flipped channels on her TV, she heard a remark by Oprah Winfrey, "The key to life is being guided by your heart." She took Oprah's comment as an assuring word that God would work through her heart—through her intuition—and steer her toward wholeness. Many times the heart will remain steady when the mind is shaky..

But for God to steer us, we must be moving. A ship that is "dead" in the water can't be turned around—and neither can we.

All men (and women) may not *be* equal, but we all have equal opportunity through prayer with God's help.

In life many times, it is just you and God. God enables the "naturals" to do the supernatural, and uses the ordinary people to accomplish the extraordinary. There are no great people, only great challenges that ordinary people are forced by circumstances to meet. A variation on an old Chinese proverb comes to mind, "Woman who says it cannot be done, should not interrupt woman who is doing it." King David learned that God was the one who was able to restore his soul. He doesn't restore good as new, like new, but *all new*.

To be in tune with ourselves, we may have to cut some things out of our lives. I have one relative whose days are filled with bland routines and blah people. She is completely preoccupied with her organized rut and refuses to deviate from it. I doubt that, if her husband died, she would have time to attend the funeral. She would do well to follow this admonition: "Always do what you can't always do." Use your imagination. Break out of dead routines and self-imposed deadlocks.

When I was growing up, teen girls idolized Veronica Lake. She wore her hair coyly over her eyes. I wanted to be like her, but my mother had other ideas. One day my mother said, "Either you cut your bangs, or I will cut them for you." And sometimes I think that's how God works with us.

He wants to restore our souls, He wants us to "run and not be weary," "walk and not faint," even "mount up with wings as eagles" (see Isaiah 40:31). But sometimes He asks that we "work out [our] own salvation with fear and trembling" (Philippians 2:12); He asks that we "cut our own bangs" or to put it another way, clean out the corners of our lives. We may try to *cut* corners. Our lives may look tidy and clean but we can be hiding clutter that keeps us from satisfaction, and keeps us out of tune with life itself. Remember, women who may be kept from great temptations can be overwhelmed and overcome by incessant small ones. It's not always the mountain in my path that makes life unbearable, but the discomfort of the little stones in my shoe.

Four Dead Ends

Let's look at a few thought patterns that can sap our energy:

1. *Dwelling on past mistakes* is a draining activity. We deplete our inner resources when we worry and fret over "regrets" or being misunderstood. Even when we do our best we will be misunderstood at times. We will come to the end of a day and

gasp, "Oh, if only I could retract what I said, if only I could turn the clock back and start over."

Looking back now, the following episode seeems humorous. Not so then.

When Carl first became campus pastor at Trinity College, April was five. One day she asked her daddy for some money, and he said, "I'll let you earn some. If you will take your red wagon and pick up the beer cans in the ditch between here and the Bible school, I'll give you five cents for each can." We lived a quarter of a mile from the college and she went to work. She was gone a couple of hours, and Carl thought she'd gotten distracted playing with friends. But when April finally came into the house, she pulled Carl by the hand to the back steps where she had piled a mountain of beer cans. He thought she would find fifteen or twenty. But they counted 76. Now I wish the story ended there, but while Carl was in the dining room paying her, the back doorbell rang. It was a pastor from a local church who had come by to talk about the ministerial assocation. He gave a long hard look at those beer cans. Carl never thought to explain.

A few days later a rumor got started around town (population 2,000) that Rev. Malz had a serious drinking problem. Carl is a teetotaler. There was no way we could march the streets trying to explain. We had to put the day behind us and let what we knew carry us through what they *thought* they knew.

In our hearts we knew we were innocent. We were in tune with ourselves and couldn't allow ourselves to panic about "if onlys."

Time always marches forward, never backward. Now if our apologies and confessions are necessary to set our relationships right—with God and other people—we must stop and do what we can to right our wrongs. There's one quick cure for guilt: Get down on your knees and let the blood of Jesus wash you clean. Get down on your knees, then get up on yourself—too much introspection can result in self-centeredness and low-self-esteem. You may be down on yourself, but after He washes you clean you are worthy. Then you can turn around and walk with time into the future.

Jesus said, "Sufficient unto the day is the evil thereof" (Matthew 6:34), as a reminder that we aren't to worry about our tomorrows. But I can't help but think that He also meant that we aren't to worry about our pasts, that we are to live *one* day at a time—and that day is always today.

2. *Harboring an unforgiving spirit* also saps a woman's energy; nurse a hurt, lose your strength.

The famous musical team Gilbert and Sullivan once got into an argument over the color of the carpet in the studio they shared. So much for working in harmony; they did not speak to each other for years. For the rest of their lives they communicated by writing, sending words and lyrics back and forth. They depleted so much energy on unresolved conflict. Think what they might have accomplished if they could have shaken hands and put the past behind them.

It isn't always easy to forgive offenses that have caused great pain, but it must be done. Forgiving is a matter of spiritual surgery—slicing out a cancer that has to go if we are to remain healthy and in tune.

Most Christians have memorized the Lord's Prayer which includes the line "Forgive us our debts, as we forgive our debtors" (Matthew 6:12). That line implies that God will forgive us *only* as we forgive others. But Jesus didn't leave it there. He ended his prayer with "Amen," and then immediately continued His teaching with this: "If ye forgive men their trespasses, your

101

heavenly Father will also forgive you: But if ye forgive not men their trespasses, neither will your Father forgive your trespasses" (verses 14–15). Clearly, we must forgive those who have wounded us if we are ever to receive God's cleansing forgiveness of ourselves.

In my reading I came across this line: "He who refuses to forgive, breaks the bridge over which he himself must pass."

Although forgiveness is in a sense spiritual surgery, it is not surgery we must perform on ourselves. What we must do, though, is sign the "release papers." We must be willing to let go of our grudge and give God permission to cut out the cancer. Sometimes we perversely want to hold onto our anger. God says, "Let go, let go." How much we are harming ourselves, how much energy we are wasting—trying to hold onto a little piece of poison. Release it to God in prayer. State out loud unequivocally, "I forgive _____ for his/her action that hurt me." Then ask God to change the feelings in your heart from bitterness to peace.

3. A *lack of goals* can drain off our energy so that the days and weeks slip away, like water down a pipe. Although God calls us to live today to its fullest and not *worry* about tomorrow, it is a foolish person who doesn't look ahead and reach toward a goal. In her book *You Can Make Your Dreams Come True* Dale Hanson Bourke says that "life is a delicate balance between planned activities and unexpected circumstances. It is our job to plan for the future, make the most of what we have, and say yes to opportunity."

Any runner knows the value of having an end destination in mind. The apostle Paul used the goal image when he spoke of his own spiritual life: "Forgetting what is behind and straining toward what is ahead, I press on toward the goal to win the prize . . ." (Philippians 3:13–14, NIV).

Reaching a goal, even a little one that seems inconsequential to anyone but yourself, gives a spurt of energy—as if it were adrenalin. But there's something slightly elusive about goals. If they're never set, they can't be reached; dreams never dreamt can't come true.

Before he started sketching pictures of birds, James Audubon sat in jail because he couldn't pay his debts. But he had a driving desire to paint birds and at age thirty-five he started the series that won him world renown. His desire was his strength. He said, "Completing my work keeps my spirit at par."

4. *Unconquered habits* can emotionally and physically drain us. Bad habits come in all shapes and sizes but one in particular comes to my mind—that of gluttony.

Gluttony is probably the first personal sin. If we can discipline this area of our lives, control often comes easily in other areas. Proverbs 23:19–21 has some strong warnings: "Listen, my son, and be wise. . . . Do not join those who drink too much wine or gorge themselves on meat, for drunkards and gluttons become poor, and drowsiness clothes them in rags" (NIV).

For more than a hundred years, the church has talked a lot about temperance—which is one of the fruits of the Spirit—as if it were linked exclusively to the word *alcohol*, but it's not. We're to be temperate in all things including what we eat. And being temperate always starts with being self-controlled.

The apostle Paul makes a point of saying that our bodies—not our minds or souls or spirits—are temples of the Holy Spirit (1 Corinthians 6:19). In the next verse he commands, "Therefore honor God with your body." In the context of this passage, Paul is referring to our sexuality but I think he presents a principle that applies to the manner in which we tend our bodies.

Have you ever stopped and talked to a serious gardener about his or her land and the crop yield? Gardeners are careful to feed their soil the right nutrients so the harvest will be as perfect as they can make it. Likewise, to be at our best, to be in tune with ourselves, we must take proper care of our bodies, including our diet.

While I was writing *Angels Watching Over Me* I gained about thirty pounds. Twenty-two of them slipped up on me in one month between Thanksgiving and Christmas. It's easy for me to rationalize how this happened. My family brags on my goodies. To me, their comments are like spurs in the sides of a running horse. The more they complimented me, the more I baked—and ate. But, also, I sat for long hours at the typewriter, exercising nothing but my brain and my fingers. As they say, inch by inch anything's a cinch. Well, inch by inch I outgrew my wardrobe.

I wished Carl or someone with a magic wand could have said a few words and made those pounds disappear. But it doesn't happen that way. I had to take my own body and get it under control.

Carl also came to a turning point. On his fortieth birthday, he walked out of a shower and looked at his naked body in the mirror. Right then and there he said, "I refuse to live in this ugly shell the rest of my life." He started walking, running, riding a bicycle, and cut his eating portions in half. Since then he has lost sixty-five pounds and has kept them off.

I attended the funeral of a writer friend of mine. In his sermon the minister said, "As it has pleased God to take our sister . . . ." God did not *take* her! How easy it is to blame a lot of things on the devil and/or God. That woman killed herself with her mouth. She ate a lot—the wrong things. She worried too much, and she talked too much. Much of the stress that caused her fatal heart attack was brought on by sixty excess pounds and a brash, opinionated criticism that had boomeranged and caused her so much remorse that she couldn't sleep.

Are we realistic, or do we embroider things to make them appealing to us?

There are some excellent books with weight control suggestions by professionals. If you need a little boost, here are some from women I know who have trimmed down successfully.

One friend who struggled with her diet put a large black "X" on her right hand as a reminder that it was the culprit that was putting the food in her mouth and ruining the size of her body. In a way that "X" served as her own personalization of Psalm 141:3: "Set a watch, O, Lord, before my mouth; keep the door of my lips." It also served to spur her on when people asked about it. She would acknowledge that it was a means by which she hoped to regain self-control. Her doctor suggested that women should never consume more bulk at any meal than what is taken up by their hands in a praying hands position (approximately ten ounces).

This same doctor had one patient who set her alarm clock at 7:00 A.M., 12:00 noon, and 5:00 P.M. Then—and only then—did she eat. In between, she refused to consume anything but water.

I know another woman who lost eighty pounds by going on a "no white" diet: no gravy, no pasta, no white bread, no sugar—nothing white.

My husband was in Egypt for some time. The diet there consisted mainly of raw fruit, raw vegetables, fish, nuts, cheese, and some chicken, and he was amazed at how lean, healthy, and strong Egyptian women seemed to be.

April picked up some weight in her first year of college. But she has trimmed off eighteen pounds by eating her last meal at 5:00 P.M. and it is just a salad with grated cheese on top.

When it comes to your diet, remember your attitude is in charge. Don't dabble. Plunge. Even if yesterday was one long picnic, start over—now. Put the past behind you and ask God for new strength to control your diet—today.

Remember, *food is not fun. It is fuel for strength to do worthwhile things.* Exercise is essential.

Your Strength

There's a wonderful verse in Isaiah: "In quietness and in confidence shall be your strength" (30:15). There is nothing more powerful than a tender, "in-tune" woman, and nothing more obnoxious than a religious, mouthy shrew full of emotional hysteria in the name of anointed power. You may consider yourself educated, qualified, but God rarely uses a nervous, uptight vessel. He may bypass it for a relaxed, natural, sensitive, and simple woman who is confident in herself and in her God. You can sense a woman's true nature not by what she says but by what she does. Actions speak louder than words.

The Lord uses the "always" people, the "in-the-meantime" women. Only as a last resort does He use a see-saw, teeter-totter, pendulum personality, the "I need someone who can reason with force" person.

Some women are merely assertive without something to be assertive about. A female can talk softly if she has the power of self-respect. Eating or speaking, our *attitudes are in charge.* The woman most secure in a high position is usually one who would gladly be a subject. She commands best who can obey. She speaks surely who would gladly keep silent.

God will use a willing heart and mind in a woman's own sphere of influence. Jesus never pushed to promote Himself. As many as came to Him, He received them. If you're in tune with God and people, you don't need a promotional agent. God will put you where He wants you.

Recently when I was in Cincinnati, Ohio, a man approached me and asked if he could be my promotional director. I quietly opened my Bible and read to him Psalm 75:6–7: " 'Promotion cometh neither from the east, nor the west, nor from the south. But God . . . putteth down one, and setteth up another.' Promotion comes from the Lord." He smiled and tried again. "Perhaps you would let me be your agent. I could get you into large auditoriums, some important places. I represent many religious celebrities and we'd both make a lot of money. I would charge you fifteen percent of your offerings."

I tried not to grin, and stated my case in a different way: "I have an agent, and He charges only ten percent."

The man understood. I tithe ten percent of my income to God's work, most of it to Trinity Bible College to train Christian ministers, missionaries, teachers, and educators.

Look at the biblical story of Queen Esther. She did not rely on promotional gimmicks; she relied on a quiet inner strength given to her by the God in whom she put her trust. When Esther was young, she was brought into the king's harem. She knew the king was looking for a queen but she did not scheme to try to get that position. The Scripture says, "Anything she wanted was given her to take with her from the harem to the king's palace. . . . When the turn came for Esther . . . to go to the king, she asked for nothing other than what Hegai, the king's eunuch who was in charge of the harem, suggested. And Esther won the favor of everyone who saw her" (Esther 2:13–15, NIV).

That everyone included the king, who put a crown on her head. But that's not the end of the story. There seems to be a reason she was made queen. As her cousin later said of her, "Who knows but that you have come to royal position for such a time as this?" (4:14). What was the crisis that prompted Mordecai's question? The king's right-hand man, Haman, had persuaded the king to decree that all the Jewish population would be killed.

Now, in the time of crisis, Esther's inner strength became most evident. Although it was against the law for her to enter the king's presence unbidden, she did so after having fasted and prayed for three days. (Closet prayer is like the footing of a skyscraper—underground, unseen, unnoticed but essential for the large structure to stand.) The biblical account is wonderfully sparse: "On the third day Esther put on her royal robes and stood in the inner court of the palace, in front of the king's hall. The king was sitting on his royal throne in the hall, facing the entrance. When he saw Queen Esther standing in the court, he was pleased with her and held out to her the gold scepter that was in his hand. So Esther approached and touched the tip of the scepter" (5:1–2, NIV).

Her quiet boldness—undergirded by days of prayer—saved her whole nation.

Esther's story hasn't been preserved as Scripture by accident. With no fanfare she walked into the presence of the king saying, "If I perish, I perish" (4:16).

I wish I'd known that woman! She followed three basic rules: Proceed with caution, walk softly, talk softly.

Think about it. Who is the Christian woman who has had the greatest impact on your life? Usually it's not one who raves, rants, roars, and bellows, but a consistent woman who possesses integrity and quiet power, through prayer.

In Touch With Reality

Our quiet strength comes when we look up to God at the same time we have our feet planted on the ground. We need to be sensitive, but not gullible. Jesus said, "Abide [take up residence] in Me . . . and "Let My words abide [take up residence] in you." I meet so many women who are unplugged from current reality, disconnected from God, pulled away from the source. I call them "Square Halos." Mark Twain said, "It ain't ignorance that hurts a person, but knowing too much that ain't the truth."

When I was a dormitory supervisor at Central Bible College in Springfield, Missouri, I was housemother for 336 great students; well, that is, 334 were great, but two of them made me think that not all the "kookies" are in the jar. These two women kept coming to my office each telling me that God had told them that a certain young ministerial student was to be their husband. I couldn't tell one about the other for fear of hateful competition, but both of these women declared they were the helpmeet for the same guy.

They both asked me to approach him and introduce them. Now I'm no Solomon, but I specialize in females since the children I've raised have all been daughters. I decided to write the male student a note requesting he come to my office in the afternoon. I also left a note in each of the girls' boxes, asking them to come the following morning—at different times—so I could report the result of my conference with the soon-to-be reverend.

My meeting with him wasn't lengthy, as he quietly told me that he saw things yet a third way. He was engaged to be married to a woman back home in Kansas. Needless to say, there were crestfallen looks the next morning as their false ideas of reality caved in.

Now faith is the evidence of things not seen (Hebrews 11:1). Time has a way of proving whether our faith is grounded in illusion or in God and His truth.

I attended a women's volleyball game where the Christian college team was being badly beaten. At halftime I put an arm around the captain to encourage her. She shrugged my sympathy with a "Don't worry, Betty. We'll win. Jesus is on our team!" That may have been true, but I don't believe He was playing that night. They lost miserably. There was an illusionary quality to her faith that in time was evident.

Don't misunderstand me. I do believe in miracles. We serve a God of the supernatural.

The virginal conception of Jesus was naturally impossible. It was an "unreal reality." Mary conceived of the Holy Ghost, but she brought forth a flesh-and-blood child, not a spook. Time proved her revelation a reality.

Len LeSourd taught me something eight years ago that applies to writing. But I'm now learning that it also applies to my life as a whole. "Less is more," he said. "Sometimes what you leave out of a book is more important than what you put in."

Probably eighty percent of the women I meet don't leave anything out. They talk as if they've been vaccinated with a phonograph needle. In contrast, consider what the Gospels say about Mary. The angel of the Lord spoke, told her some amazing news about what would happen to her and she pondered it in her heart. She obviously could keep a secret. I believe God would show women more today if He could trust them to keep a secret and allow His actions to prove themselves.

If we remain practical, in tune with ourselves and God, God will make up the difference. The supernatural is His department, His speciality. The natural is ours.

6
Out of Tune

The story you are about to hear is true; the name has not been changed to protect the guilty, namely me.

I have experienced the ultimate satisfaction of being in tune, but I have suffered the unavoidable consequences of being out of tune.

No one can *make* you happy. Happy is something you are. In contrast, a woman can make herself sick.

I did not want to be a pastor's wife. I had been a pastor's daughter. The unrealistic expectations, mostly self-imposed, began to build up inside me when Carl took a pastorate. I suffered silently for three years with a stiff neck and pains in the vertebrae of my upper back. I was shocked at the diagnosis when a fine physician of a renowned clinic suggested, "Mrs. Malz, you must either change your attitude toward your job, or change jobs."

He prescribed medication, we experimented with therapy by methods of heat pack, traction of my neck and chin, and special exercises. I was anointed and prayed for according to the method of divine healing prescribed in St. James, chapter five, by three internationally known evangelists and my husband in our local, praying church.

After a few years, I gave up, discontinued medication and tried to learn to live with it. When I sat at a typewriter long hours, it hurt like a toothache in your neck. When I drove I had to turn my entire body to look sideways because the vertebrae had frozen where the cushions between had deteriorated. The enemy of my spirit tried to plague my positive attitude by accusation: "Yes, you write about, tell about miracles, and others receive. But you still are suffering after twelve long years." I have had so much mercy in my lifetime that if I never receive anything else from God I will write ten books of His faithfulness; yet my neck hurt. But, a prayer that ascends to the golden throne room of God like a laser beam or airport beacon never loses its energy, though we may sometimes ourselves get out of tune.

A young pastor asked me to come to a remote little town in upper Maine and tell my story to a small congregation. I started to say no, since we were packing to move. I tuned in to God through simple, quiet prayer, and my spirit told me yes.

When I arrived the little church was full, so I sat by the pastor's wife on the front row until I was introduced. I felt a tap, tap, tap on my left shoulder. Looking around I saw a pitifully retarded young woman of about thirty-five, her facial features distorted, and that faraway look in her eyes. She was wearing silver-colored rubber moon boots and a turquoise sweatsuit with her name printed on it on Sunday morning! It was plain to see that she was out of tune with reality not to mention being out of tune with trend and style. She kissed my cheek and said, "I like you." It tore me up. I hugged her and replied, "I like you too, Ruthie."

When I was introduced I had a hard time starting. I had ridden in the back of a car almost all night to get to that remote location, and the back of my osteoarthritic neck was "killing me."

Little Ruthie stood up and declared, "I like her." When the people realized that I was not disturbed I could tell they liked me, too.

I said yes to the Lord when he impressed me to lay aside my stale notes and relate the simple message to the people, "Invest in people. Love people. The only commodity that transfers to eternity, the only thing you can take with you is people." I felt love begin to flow between myself and those people. Ruthie stood up again. She was out of tune with procedure, but in tune with genuine love. She had tears in her eyes when she said, "I like this place!" For the next twenty minutes communication was simple, easy, and genuine.

At the close of the service when the pastor gave the invitation, five people received Jesus as Savior and prayed the sinner's prayer.

When I sat back down on the front row, my neck hurt worse, and my spine began to convulse. I had not complained, not even told people about the pain for years. I had resigned, given up. Then, gently, I felt little fingers touch the top of my head. They moved down my back, tracing all five vertebrae down to the last one that ached. The pain was gone, my head could turn easily, freely. God had used an instrument of healing that seemed out of tune with reality, in tune to love (God *is* love). This only happened three weeks ago! I cannot explain it. God in His overruling, practical, superintending providence used a homely instrument, an atmosphere of love in which people invested in people, to bring about my healing. I can turn my head freely and without any discomfort for the first time in twelve years!

Saying yes to God is "fine-tuning." Investing in people is a two-way street. Stretch your imagination with me for a few more lines:

Elijah said yes and the barrel of meal never did run over, but it never did run out!

Moses said yes at the Red Sea and 160,000 people walked through on a dry path!

God took His Son aside from the golden throne room and appointed Him a task. And because of His love for people Jesus said yes. He eradicates our sin. He heals us, and when the world gets unbearable, He will come to take us to the new earth where we will experience the place we have been programmed to go since the day we were born!

7

In Tune with Change

"I am the Lord, I change not."

Malachi 3:6

Most people bellyache at change. They hate the first step of the race of growth; they love the end result, the trophy, but resent the steps in-between. When things get difficult we're too apt to yell, "Stop. Everything's moving too fast."

But women who are in tune with God needn't be out of tune with change—whether it be the kind that is like a hurricane (you have a warning that it's coming) or the kind that's like a tornado (you're surprised that it touches down so quickly and does so much damage).

Expected Life Changes

Most of us can anticipate planned progression. When we know what the next step is and when we know that next step will be rewarding, we're eager for change.

My "baby" niece Shanda is turning sixteen. She recently said, "Aunt Betty, I get my braces off in twelve more days." She could hardly wait. She will emerge with a transformed smile, and she is blooming into a lovely woman. She is moving to the driver's seat (literally, as she's getting a driver's license) and she's changing the decor of her bedroom from pastel butterflies to a music motif—black and white with bright pink accents.

That kind of change at that age is exciting. But our attitudes about life change as we pass through stages of development. In our twenties we say, "I should," in our thirties, "I want," and in our forties, "I must!" Although I say this, I don't think we should take the psychologists' theories of stages too seriously. Only machines work by units, only bureaucracy works step by step. Christians, thank God, have an individual inner dynamic that can never be precisely coded. Some of us are jerked to the next stage of development by tragedy or some other sudden unexpected lurch. Some even skip stages and grow up too soon.

Yet as the birthday celebrations add up, we no longer anticipate change because we fear the future may not include progression but regression.

My own mother hated change. For a year she dreaded our impending move to Florida. But after we got here, she was "the biggest duck in the puddle." She was offered jobs with *four* real estate firms. She found out how well she could sell the Sunshine State.

It's okay to be afraid of change, to quake, rattle, shake, and rumble. You may even wobble from one stage of life to another. Sometimes that initial fear can make us stop and ask questions that we otherwise would skip by. Ruth Denny explained that as she entered menopause she had a lot of physical difficulties. When her gynecologist suggested a hysterectomy, Ruth said,

"Not so fast. How would you like someone to cut out your hormones?"

The doctor raised his eyebrows and Ruth went to prayer. She asked others to pray with her and Jesus healed her, brought her quickly through the "change of life."

At a point when the children are gone and many women would be asking, "Is this all there is?" Ruth has developed a ministry of prayer and understanding for women going through menopause. (Her address is listed along with those of other support people in the appendix on page 189.)

When procreation ceases, a new kind of creativity can be released. A woman's narrow existence (Mama Bear serving Papa Bear and 2.6 baby bears), can open up to new challenges. Years ago, Catherine Marshall cautioned me, "Betty, don't try to do everything in your thirties. Wait until the kids are grown." She knew that the children needed my early years, but that I'd need new challenges later in my life. Unfortunately, this surge of energy in a woman often comes about the time a husband feels his power and his dreams slipping away. A wife is likely brimming with creative ambition to climb her own mountain, just when a husband is ready to relax and read the newspaper at the summer house. It is strange, but two people don't usually develop mentally or spiritually at the same pace. They're seldom in perfect step with each other. But if a husband and wife stay in tune with each other, they can help each other change and grow.

On Clearwater, Florida's, Channel 22 Herman Bailey hosts a telecast "Action Sixties." His wife, Sharron, directs the program and recently shared her own determination to stay atuned to her husband while he went through a mid-life crisis, a drastic physical and emotional change between the ages of fifty and sixty. She admitted, "If I had left and he had come through it a better man (which he admits he has), then some other women would have taken credit, claimed the glory for the 'new Herman.' " As I heard her story I was reminded that there is a reward to the "always" people, the "in-the-meantime" woman. If both parties develop an interest in each other and switch to a general interest it can be a wonderfully rewarding change.

Remember, a lobster grows by developing and shedding a series of hard, protective shells. The oyster's pearl is formed by a covering a grain of sand—working "against the grain." We must learn to s-t-r-e-t-c-h.

If there's one thing that's constant about life it's the reality of change. Life is a constant struggle. Many people harbor the notion, "Once I get through this, life will be smooth sailing." But that's just when something else comes along to remind us that the world is ever turning.

Solomon knew about the reality of change and modern folk songwriters made our whole generation aware of his timeless words: "There is a time for everything, and a season for every activity under heaven: a time to be born and a time to die, a time to plant and a time to uproot, a time to kill and a time to heal, a time to tear down and a time to build, a time to weep and a time to laugh . . ." (Ecclesiastes 3:1–4, NIV).

When I moved away from the Clearwater, Florida, area years ago, Crystal Beach was a sleepy village of fishermen. It is still one of the unspoiled spots on the Gulf coast. But how it has grown, developed. They say that the road to progress is always under construction. I have changed since I last visited here. I used to enjoy living in the snow and coming here for a vacation. Now, I enjoy living here and going to the snow for a vacation.

Traumatic Change: Death

Although some change comes slowly, like a hurricane, some comes like a tornado, dipping down at unexpected times and attacking us. We shudder at these surprises that interrupt our routines and change the course of our lives.

When Lynne DeGroot was thirteen, her parents and grandparents, out for a ride, were hit broadside. Lynne's mom lived seven hours. Her dad and both maternal grandparents were dead on arrival at the hospital.

At first, denial helped absorb the shock. The closed coffins made the deaths seem unreal. She says it wasn't until she saw the names listed on a schedule board at the funeral home that reality really sank in. She allowed herself to grieve but determined that she would be strong. *I will make it somehow*, she told herself, *and life will go on.*

Her aunt and uncle, a minister, took Lynne and her ten-year-old sister, Kim, home with them to Michigan. They couldn't take the place of the girls' real parents, but showered the girls with love.

The uncle comforted them, "Both your father and mother were teachers and taught you always to complete your assignments. They evidently completed theirs early."

Lynne knew her parents were with their Lord and says, "I refused to let the things I didn't understand rob me of what I did understand." And she did understand Romans 8:28: "All things work together for good to them that love God."

Lynne is now a calm, poised student at Wheaton College. Her parents' insurance money is allowing her to train to be a high school social science teacher and a softball coach. Eventually she wants to be a professional counselor of adolescents so she can help kids who are hurting, as she was.

When Lynne looks back on the day that so dramatically changed her life she can see beyond the tears she once shed. "My dad always had cars in bad repair, clunkers," she remembers. "And the hearse—taking him for his last ride to the cemetery— had a flat tire. Just like life."

I believe if we can look ahead of our present circumstances we can smile and have faith for the long-range program.

I don't think anyone is *totally* prepared for death to strike a loved one, even when the warning signs are clear.

I was only thirty-four when my first husband died. I knew he was going in for heart surgery, so I was somewhat prepared for the physical risk involved. I now would be even more prepared by following these ten guidelines that can help insulate women from the physical trauma of a husband's death or disablement.

1. Establish credit in both spouses' names.
2. Increase the limits on credit cards as a source of standby cash.
3. Arrange with your bank for a personal line of credit that provides access to a guaranteed amount of emergency cash.
4. Know where family records and documents are stored and keep a set of copies elsewhere.
5. Make a list of life insurance policies. Do not keep them

in a safe-deposit box because many states seal the box as soon as a death certificate is signed.

6. Arrange for a standby power of attorney to be activated if either spouse becomes ill or disabled.

7. Be sure both spouses know who family advisors are.

8. Be certain you have a disability insurance. Only three percent of last year's mortgage foreclosures were due to death, while 47 percent resulted from serious illness or disability.

9. Write a will and update it yearly. Be sure your selections of guardian and financial disbursement for your children continue to be viable. If you do not name them, the state decides who gets your children, not your relatives.

10. Take photographs of every room in your house so that in case of fire or theft a complete proof and accounting can be given to the insurance company to collect for replacement.

Despite these preparations that can reduce the physical devastation caused by the "tornado" of death or disablement, there is no one so lost in spirit as a woman who has just lost a loving mate.

The first time I heard the classical piece "The Merry Widow Waltz," I thought a more incongruous title could hardly be imagined.

One woman who lost a husband to death immediately turned to Isaiah 54. "Thou shalt forget the shame of thy youth, and shalt not remember the reproach of thy widowhood any more. For thy Maker is thine husband; the Lord of hosts is his name" (verses

4 –5). Her grief was tempered by those assuring words. Her loss was made easier knowing that God was at her side during her upheaval.

Another woman, recently recovered from grief over the death of a son, told me how she'd struggled to get in tune with change. To live in the present she had to let go of the past. She said, "After two years of chronic, prolonged mourning, my heart was torn between the fear of letting go of the grief and a desire to be free from its heavy burden." As she prayed the Lord revealed that He wanted to bear her sorrow and grief for her. At first she resisted, saying, "Lord, You took my son, now you want my grief, too? It's not fair. It's all I have left of him!" It never occurred to her that grief was something to be sacrificed, offered up. But for her that's what freedom involved—a deliberate letting go of the pain and the past.

As they face change, most women depend on prayer, Bible reading, meetings, their experience, Christian books. But the final answer is always *Christ Himself.* The simplicity of truth is who He is. *He* is our Peace. He is our Rock. Rely on His peace, His poise and His strength. Peace is a Person, Jesus; poise is a Person, Jesus; strength is a Person, Jesus.

As we practice the presence of God, we must remember that He is the great *I AM.* He is Emmanuel—God with us.

What else does the Bible say about our God? Unlike our lives, which are ever turning and churning, the God who is in control of our lives is utterly steadfast. James 1:17 says that He "does not change like shifting shadows" (NIV). King James says with Him there "is no variableness, neither shadow of turning." Malachi 3:6 says, "I am the Lord, I change not." And Hebrews 13:8 says, "Jesus Christ the same yesterday, and to-day, and for ever."

And what precedes this verse in Hebrews? Verse 5 of the same chapter says, "I will never leave thee, nor forsake thee." Read backward it means the same!

A Call for Balance

When my stepdaughter Connie went through the pain of divorce, her world—even our world—was shaken. I must admit that we reacted badly. Carl was angry. Our family had never been touched by divorce; we didn't "deserve" this. Living in a small town which revolves around the college Carl administered, we were embarrassed. We felt like running away, or putting sacks over our heads when we drove to the grocery store.

But we have learned that we must be tuned in to change. We discovered that seventy-six percent of the American population is directly or indirectly affected by divorce. We realized that Aimee Semple McPherson who incorporated the International Church of the Foursquare Gospel and Katherine Kuhlman, the instrument of healing to millions, both suffered failed marriages. Divorce is not the unforgivable sin.

Connie is no stranger to change. She was born in India and raised on the mission field. By the time she had grown she had gone to twelve different schools. When she came back here to the States she entered a totally foreign culture even though she was, in a sense, returning "home." When she was only thirteen she watched her mother die of cancer, and several years later she had to adjust to life with a stepmother—me. But all too soon, she was married—and the mother of three children, including a lively pair of twins. As if that hadn't been enough major change for one lifetime, she's since undergone four brain-tumor surgeries, thank God, successfully.

When I asked her to write down what she's learned about coping with her most recent upheaval, she shared the following that I'd like to pass on to you:

"I know what pain feels like. It can range from an inner raging burning to a sadness that hides behind a mask of coping.

"Sometimes I cry because the lessons are hard and I grow weary. But in my pain I carry the very reason for Jesus' coming to earth. I cannot save myself from the torment of this life. Rather, His strength is as deep as my weakness.

"A completed Christian woman lives in life in *balance*. She knows that the intimate relationship she has with Jesus will counteract all the outward circumstances that would seek to take her eyes off the faithfulness of God.

"Crisis changes can seem to be for destruction, but God faithfully brings His glory to the situation. Our understanding and logical evaluation of life are so limited. Oftentimes, we fail to see good. God's eyes see so much more.

"For a Christian this world is not reality . . . for our home is beyond this flesh and blood. The crisis is not true reality, but seeing the Christ behind the crisis is! This truth is so simple yet so hard to keep. The crisis and pain you're going through are only real to a point because Christ, the Person, beyond the crisis, is the comfort.

"Looking back over my life I see it was not I who changed all the questions into peace and trust, rest and convictions. Rather, it was God's good will to reveal Himself. The balance gained after crisis will come as you turn your eyes off the circumstances and onto the face of your precious Jesus—a daughter turning to her Father-Creator in childlike faith and trust that He will see her through all things. Jesus

125

was not a man of pat answers, but one of intimate sharing relationships. He has not changed.

"The feeling of losing one's balance is terrifying; for that particular moment there seems to be no control over where you might land. But place your eyes on our Lord and lean not to your own understanding of the ending of the story; you're only at the beginning.

"When I start to panic and feel as if life is out of control, I remind myself of three principles:

"1. *Take* one day at a time, sometimes one moment at a time. Don't lean on the past or place your securities in your own future plans. Look only to God and trust that He will make His path plain. The feelings of disorder will not last, and basing your understanding of circumstances on your emotions may keep you from seeing the future through eyes of faith.

"2. *Give* one day at a time. Instead of thrusting toward some future ministry, occupy your hands today. Look at your own family and give them your best. Oftentimes it's at-home loving, forgiving, and learning that prepares us for future challenges.

"3. *Be* one day at a time. Realize that the love of your Creator goes beyond your works. Dare to trust Him without feeling you have to accumulate an impressive list of 'I've dones.' "

Why did I ask Connie to share what she's learned as she's repeatedly faced major upheavals? Through her painful ordeals she's learned the importance of staying in tune with change.

A Lesson in Contrasts

Earlier I mentioned the story of Ruth and Naomi, two widows who traveled from Moab to Bethlehem to make a new life for themselves. Although it seems that Naomi eventually gained a healthy perspective on life, she arrived in Bethlehem in severe straits. Ruth 1 says, "When they arrived in Bethlehem, the whole town was stirred because of them, and the women exclaimed, 'Can this be Naomi?' 'Don't call me Naomi [which means Pleasant],' she told them. "Call me Mara [Bitter], because the Almighty has made my life very bitter. I went away full, but the Lord has brought me back empty" (verses 19–21, NIV).

Now there was one temporarily out-of-tune woman, who had her eyes fixed on her own circumstances rather than on her steadfast Lord.

In contrast, the first chapter of Job ends with Job receiving word that his children had been killed by a tornado and his livelihood—his oxen, donkeys, sheep, and camels—had been stolen or killed. How did Job respond? He grieved—he tore his robe and shaved his head—and he fell to the ground and said, "The Lord gave and the Lord has taken away; may the name of the Lord be praised" (Job 1:21, NIV). Job's pain was real but it never broke his spirit; it never caused him to lose his perfect pitch.

Recently I found this poem by A. B. Simpson, founder of the Christian and Missionary Alliance denomination. He obviously knew where his hope lay—in Jesus, the One in whom there is no shadow of turning.

HIMSELF

Once it was the blessing,
Now it is the Lord.
Once it was the feeling,
Now it is His Word.
Once His gifts I wanted,
Now the Giver own;
Once I sought for healing,
Now Himself alone.

Once 'twas painful trying,
Now 'tis perfect trust;
Once a half salvation,
Now the uttermost.
Once 'twas ceaseless holding,
Now He holds me fast;
Once 'twas constant drifting,
Now my anchor's cast.

Once 'twas busy planning,
Now 'tis trustful prayer;
Once 'twas anxious caring,
Now He has the care.
Once 'twas what I wanted,
Now what Jesus says;
Once 'twas constant asking,
Now 'tis ceaseless praise.

Once it was my working,
His it hence shall be;
Once I tried to use Him,
Now He uses me.
Once the power I wanted,
Now the Mighty one;

Once for self I labored,
Now for Him alone.

Once I hoped in Jesus,
Now I know He's mine;
Once my lamps were dying,
Now they brightly shine.
Once for death I waited,
Now His coming hail;
And my hopes are anchored,
Safe within the vail.

8

Creative Aging

In a town of 2,000 everyone notices the newcomer, or at least I do. And one Sunday I introduced myself to the stranger, whose name, I learned, was Hannah Hyde. Just by watching her I saw that she had lived a long time. Her white hair and aging hands were clues that she was older than I, yet she radiated energy and charm I'd seen in few women—no matter what their age. On the way out of church, she stopped at the drinking fountain in the foyer. I also paused because I wanted to get to know her. "That must be the fountain of youth," I commented. Hoping she'd understand, I continued, somewhat cryptically, "You are younger than you are." Then I got right to the point. "I'm writing a book that includes a chapter on aging. I'd love to interview you."

Immediately her dark eyes lit up. "Someday I talk to you about that," she answered in a German accent that I loved.

I learned that she was the mother-in-law of Dr. Norman

Shuert, a professor at Trinity. Monday morning I looked up the Shuerts' number and made a note to call her in the afternoon, after I got home from some errands. But my best-laid plans were preempted. Around 10:00 A.M. I was driving down Main Street in my old convertible. It was only 56 degrees, but I had the top down as it was one of the first sunny spring days. When I rounded the corner there she stood, Hannah Hyde. When she saw me she smiled and stuck out her thumb as if she were hitchhiking. Of course I stopped and offered her a lift. "I've always wanted to ride in one of these," she said.

"Then jump in," I suggested.

She hesitated just a second. "But *how* do I get in?"

"Haven't you seen the Dukes of Hazzard? You jump in."

I was teasing, but until I quickly showed her how to open it, she seemed ready and willing to leap over the low door. She's got to be one of the youngest old women I've met.

I know we all face aging and death; there's no getting around it, but this woman's personality—if not her body—seemed to have defied the aging process. It did seem she drank from a fountain of youth. Before the interview, I thought she probably had been a wealthy woman of ease all her life; the years had worn well with her because she'd never seen hardship. Well, I was wrong.

Hannah was Jewish, born in Germany. She remembers one special joy of her young childhood—the piano. But her father's business was doing poorly and one day someone came and took the piano away. To keep food on the table her father found a job, and Hannah took a job in a mercantile store. But then in 1929 things got worse. Her mother died in a flu epidemic. Her father grew sullen and depressed and hanged himself. At sixteen years of age, she was an orphan and responsible for two brothers. The older brother was retarded, and the younger brother helped by working six days a week.

Hannah fell in love with a young man who wasn't Jewish, but the government squelched their relationship. "In Germany, you didn't say no," she explained, but she lived on hope.

When she was twenty-five, she and her younger brother came to America carrying ten dollars each. They stayed with a cousin in New York, and despite her limited English she got a job taking care of a sick person.

"I never lost hope," she told me. "I dreamed of marrying an American and having a family." Her dream didn't take long to materialize; three weeks after she arrived in New York she was engaged to a man she'd just met.

They answered a newspaper ad: "Couple wanted: a butler and a cook." Although it seemed the wrong reason to marry, they did so and took the job, which turned out to be a nightmare: The employers took advantage of their inexperience. They had room and board, but very little pay and they worked from 7:00 A.M. to 10:00 P.M.

As she'd planned, she immediately sent money back to Germany to support her older brother, but within months she heard he'd died in a gas chamber. She struggled with remorse, with grief, with the adjustments to married life and a difficult work situation. But she didn't let herself give up.

When a newspaper ad beckoned, "Come to Houston and work," the Hydes did. Helped by a newcomers' organization, Hannah got a job at Sakowitz Department Store, and her husband took a Fuller Brush salesman's route. As life settled down into a routine, Hannah kept her job and raised their two daughters.

But Hannah again faced wrenching sorrow when her youngest daughter, a physical education teacher in Los Angeles, was shot and killed by an angry student. And Hannah's husband died of a brain tumor.

"Necessity kept me going," she said. As she faced widowhood she saw how much she loved life. Her father had been overcome with despair, but when Hannah developed cancer she determined that she would quit smoking—and choose life.

Hannah lived alone for fourteen years, and worked for forty-one years at Sakowitz, until the store closed its doors in downtown Houston. What would she do? she wondered. In one sense the job had been her lifeline. She loved working with young people. She had enjoyed the conversation, the friendships she made at the store, the challenge of her job.

Her daughter, Betty Ann, and Norm and their three children were Hannah's only relatives, so she decided to move to our small town and rent a little apartment four blocks away from her daughter.

Did Hannah wait for friends to come to her? No. Right from the start she looked for friends, and they loved her. She told me, "After my job was gone I needed a reason to get up each morning." She found it.

On Monday and Wednesday she volunteers her bookkeeping talent at the Bible college, where her contribution is a great asset. On Thursday you can see her at the nursing home sharing her jolly charm. The woman who was once a stranger in town quickly became one of us.

As I thought about Hannah's story, I realized, here was a woman who decided to do something besides clip coupons in her last years.

I've watched some older widowed women making wrong

choices. It doesn't seem to matter whether they have so much money they can float around the world on cruise ships or so little that they sit on a park bench feeding pigeons. Some I observe are just little old girls waiting to die. But Hannah? She worked and saved and worked again. How many women can face the challenge of a single future with charm, grace, love, and energy to spare?

The possibility of widowhood shouldn't be denied by any married woman, and I speak from experience. Although widowhood can happen at a young age, it is most likely to happen in one's later years, as we get closer to and beyond our threescore years and ten. When we are older, and especially when we are alone, we must work consciously to stay in tune with the aging process; we must work to age creatively.

As I look around me I see a number of women who, like Hannah, have chosen to reverse the curse of aging and I see some patterns in their methods: Let's look at a few of their secrets for staying in tune with aging.

Keep Giving

When I'm in Florida and want to laugh, go swimming, or ride in a top-down convertible and feel the wind in my hair, I call my Aunt Gwendolyn. She buzzes around town in her new Buick; she loves to swim, give, laugh. She loves to worship her Lord.

Some women struggle between estrogen and death. Not Aunt Gwen. Why? Because she's a giver. She gives everything but advice. She picks fruit to give away. She bakes to give away. She looks for things she can give me and do for me while I'm writing. She drives "old" people to church (she's only a great-grandmother herself). She takes in laundry for people who are too feeble to go to the laundromat—and she never charges them. I'm sure God keeps giving her health because of her giving spirit.

I've never been to Israel but one doesn't need to see the Dead Sea to understand why it is called that. Even in Jesus' time, the clear fresh Jordan River ran into the large Salt Sea and there the life-giving water grew poisonous and became the death of creatures that depended on water for life. Fish that swam into the Dead Sea soon floated to the top of it.

But things could have been different. If the terrain had allowed a river to flow out of the sea, the water would not have grown still and salty and deadly; the water would have sustained life. The Dead Sea died because it took in and never gave out, and the same principle works as we get older: we stay full of life only as we have an outlet for our service.

Keep Working

Aunt Gwen is also an example of the motto of the Sisters of Providence: "I am what I do." What does she do? She gives and she works. Something about our modern Western life makes little sense to me: While medical science has increased our lifespan, business psychology works to shrink our workspan. Some employers force their employees to retire long before their useful years are over. How ironic that President Ronald Reagan could lead our government when he wouldn't be allowed to hold any position at all in many private companies—simply because of his age.

My Aunt Gwen works four days a week, taking care of two baby great-granddaughters while their mother teaches school. Aunt Gwen gives some good advice based on her own experience. "Well-chosen mild exercise will retard the aging process. Don't compete with your younger self, but with your new self, your now self."

When Mary Laird was widowed, she was lost. Her husband's life had been hers. At first she visited her two daughters (one of them, Bobbie, is my sister-in-law). But one day she decided she must do something. If she didn't have work to do, she feared for her fate. So at seventy-two she started taking painting lessons; it was an old dream she'd let die in her younger years. Well, in a short time, she had received acclaim for her talent. I have hung several of her paintings in my home with pride. At the bottom she signs them all "Granny." The work of her hands gives me so much pleasure, I hate to think that the world might have missed her art if she hadn't seen the importance of keeping active.

And then there's Ruth Strang who was seventy when she left South Bend, Indiana, and went to teach in an orphanage in Upper Luzon, Philippines, and Mary Pallesen, a grandmother several times, who, when her husband died, went to school and got her master's degree. Now she is teaching and every summer she takes an overseas trip.

Work is also important to Berdie Kovacs. No one seems to know exactly how old she is, but she taught music to college-aged men who are now retired on Social Security—and she is still teaching music at Trinity College. When I asked her how old she was, she chuckled softly, "I'm the same age as my little finger and a little older than my teeth. I'm going on one hundred."

This summer she accompanied and directed a music group, "Redemption Singers," traveling 5,000 miles a week for ten weeks. She teaches fifteen college hours a week during the school year (considered a heavy load under any circumstances) and has twenty-one private students. She plays the organ for chapel, arranges and writes music for Dr. Bartlett Peterson, plays for weddings, funerals, and special college functions.

Berdie's husband, a violinist, died when Berdie was twenty-nine, and music and young people became her life. She has battled and won wars with leukemia and gallstones. She's a sharp dresser and few musicians have her "touch" at the organ. We almost hope the Lord lets her live forever for she can't be replaced. She has that "hurry-up feeling" of energy and seems in tune with youth, forever spring.

Keep Your Act Clean and Clear

When I asked Berdie how she fought the aging process, she said that although it is important to accept your age, it's as important to consider the advice that Zophar gave to Job: "Thou [shalt] lift up thy face without spot; yea, thou shalt be stedfast, and shalt not fear: Because thou shalt forget thy misery, and remember it as waters that pass away: And thine age shall be clearer than the noonday; thou shalt shine forth, thou shalt be as the morning. And thou shalt be secure, because there is hope; yea, thou shalt dig about thee, and thou shalt take thy rest in safety" (Job 11:15–18).

I smiled at the image "thou shalt be as the morning." It fit Berdie so perfectly.

I smiled again when she gave me three short adages that worked together to keep her young at heart.

1. *Clean out your clothes closet.* Berdie would rather have three colorful, youthful outfits than thirty frumpy ones that make her feel old. And I'd be the first to stand and witness that her tactic works. Even though I'm not sure how old she is, her

wardrobe seems to take years off her age. She said, "I coach myself to look light, look bright."

2. *Clear up your mind.* Berdie consciously makes an effort to think ahead, to think young, to think music. She wants to know what her students are thinking and to try to keep up with the times she looks to see what the latest styles are; she reads magazines that aren't published for senior citizens; she reads the newspapers and watches television.

She keeps looking ahead, planning for future years instead of dwelling in the past. She said, "I'm alone, but I refuse to emphasize what I don't have. I decided to be happy. People don't make you happy; happy is something you are. When I see a student down, I talk opposite her mood, and when I bring her up, I get up with her; thus, I keep myself up by lifting others up."

Berdie also uses Philippians 4:8 as a framework for her thought life: "Whatever is true, whatever is noble, whatever is right, whatever is pure, whatever is lovely, whatever is admirable . . . think about such things" (NIV).

3. *Clean up your speech.* Berdie says it's also important to talk young and beware of verbal traps that are dead giveaways that one is over the hill. She gave me a clipping with these examples:

1. When I was your age I used to . . .
2. I'm going to travel while I've still got my health.
3. You can't teach an old dog new tricks.
4. When you get to be my age, you'll understand.
5. Old enough to know better.
6. I'm going to take up golf while there's still time.
7. It's too new-fangled for me.

8. Well, I guess I'm good for another year.
9. At my age? Of course not!
10. I'm living on borrowed time.
11. Who wants to listen to an old duffer like me?
12. Life isn't what it used to be.
13. It's downhill from here on.
14. I don't have anymore get-up-and-go.

By the time I was through asking Berdie for her advice, I knew that her "clean and clear" act was too good to be kept as a secret.

Don't Forget the Word

My Aunt Gwen and my recently widowed mother-in-law, Dorothy Upchurch, receive great strength from the time they spend reading the Word. As Job said to his friends, "He [the Lord] would put strength in me" (Job 23:6). For these women Bible reading became a habit years ago when they were faced with the challenges that accompany youth (rules and roles) instead of those that accompany old age.

Although she's struggling with the newness of living without a mate, my mother-in-law doesn't allow herself to dwell on her own situation. Rather, she travels, visits her children and grandchildren, entertains and cooks, keeps her wardrobe in shape. But those activities that keep her busy never crowd out her time alone with her Lord—talking to Him, reading His instruction from His Word.

I've also noticed that she takes some advice of Norman Vincent Peale very seriously. He says that a good prevention for "mental erosion in the latter years" is getting an hour's sleep for every hour of creative mental activity. Dr. Peale should know, seeing as he's nearing his nineties and still active in his ministry.

Psalms 91 and 92 have some wonderful insights about staying in tune with aging: "I will set him on high, because he hath known my name . . . I will be with him in trouble; I will deliver him, and honour him. With long life will I satisfy him . . . " (Psalm 91:14 –16). "The righteous shall flourish like the palm tree: [they] . . . shall flourish in the courts of our God. They *shall still bring forth fruit in old age*" (Psalm 92:12–14).

Yesterday I drove a short distance from this cottage where I work. From the road I saw Lawrence and Sara Douglas at work in their tangerine grove. I pulled over to the shoulder and just watched them for a while. They sat together on a mini-tractor that pulled a small trailer. They talked and laughed as they looked over the beautiful heavy-laden citrus trees. Then they roamed together, past the pasture and the horses. They stopped to pick some fruit. As you might imagine, they consume a lot of fresh fruit, which both energizes them and helps keep them healthy.

The fruit of their orchard reminded me of the fruit of their lives—the fruit of their old age. Lawrence is a retired attorney and former mayor. Now both he and Sara continue to serve on committees and orchestrate projects for the betterment of the community. They stay in tune with people and their personal needs, giving dinner parties, inviting people who are going through private storms of conflict and change. During the dinners they give opportunity for guests to receive Jesus as Savior, and they pray for God to direct them with His overruling, practical, superintending providence. On occasions they anoint the sick with oil according to the method mentioned in the book of James, and Jesus does heal their friends.

Growing Real

Even before you face the reality of old age or retirement, determine that you're going to stay in tune with the aging process. How? By realizing what God can do with you. This part of the Journey can be the grandest. As you get older, you may get a physical perk from a face lift, a chin tuck, or a tummy tuck, but when you move out of yourself and into God, you will get a spiritual perk from lifting the fallen and rescuing the perishing.

Remember, every person is unique. What works for one person may not for someone else. We sometimes read too much, look to others too much for advice. We can't draw on resources we don't possess, but we must work on the raw material of God's inspiration. Follow through and follow up.

I love the story of the Velveteen Rabbit. The rabbit, a stuffed animal, wants to become real, like the skin horse. The rabbit asks the horse what it's like to be real and the horse answers, "Generally by the time you are *real* most of your hair has been loved off, your eyes drop out and you get loose in the joints and very shabby . . . but these things don't matter at all, because once you are *real*, love and are loved, you can't be ugly, except to people who don't understand."

As I see it, that's what it's like to be old—if you stay in tune with aging.

Retirement is a time for creative aging. It can be your second Genesis.

> *. . . a time to watch more sunsets*
> *to sing more*
> *pick more flowers*
> *smile more*
> *wish on more stars*
> *take more chances*
> *live more. . . .*

A Look to the Future

Unless the Lord comes first all of us will eventually face death. But for the believer, even that stage of life is an adventure.

Dr. J. T. Parish pastors a white congregation, but he has learned a great deal about life from a black shepherd and flock in the same community. The black pastor told J. T., "You whites don't face up to *real*. Death is one *real* you choose to ignore. We don't. When one of our saints approaches that final change, we call on the angels of the Lord to minister, and it is glorious. Many of them see a reception, a grand receiving line along the corridors of that golden boulevard leading to the celestial city, playing instruments and waving banners to receive the arriving newcomer to gloryland and the forever country of perfection."

Now that's how I want to go out . . . but not until I've lived to a ripe old age.

9

In Tune with Nature

"[Jesus] said to them, 'Come with me by yourselves to a quiet place and get some rest.' "

Mark 6:31, NIV

In November I received a birthday card that contained a wonderful suggestion: "Every morning lean thine arm a while upon the window sill of Heaven and gaze upon thy God. Then with that vision in thine heart, turn strong to meet the day."

This morning as the sun came up, I did just that. I rested my arms on the ledge of the east window in my kitchen. I looked toward the heavens, scanned the horizon. Like the proverbial bear, I wanted to see what I could see. As I opened my heart to the Lord, asking Him to give me strength for the day, I noticed one of his furry creatures. A gray squirrel had awakened, too, and he was in the middle of a gymnastics routine or maybe I should call it a high wire act; he was dancing elaborately on a nearby telephone wire.

The thin curtains made my window seem like a stage and what

a performance I got to see. I quickly realized the young squirrel was actually entertaining a mockingbird directly below, on the ground. Then the squirrel climbed down a telephone pole and began chasing a bluejay through the grass and across the street. Apparently a grain truck had spilled a pile of seed, and as I watched, the squirrel claimed it as his own; he climbed the little mound of grain and flicked his bushy tail, as if he were king o' the mountain.

I'm so glad I looked out and tuned in this morning; what a refreshment I could have missed.

My Father's World

Sometimes it's easy to forget that God—our Redeemer, our Provider, our Comforter—is also our Creator, not only our Creator but Creator of our world, even our cosmos. Piece by piece He put the "puzzle" in place: night and day, heaven and earth, water and dry land, grass and trees, fish and animals. Then at last He created man and woman.

God Himself obviously took pleasure in His creation, as the Genesis creation account adds, "And God saw that it was good" after the completion of each part of His handiwork.

I think God's love of nature is also evident in John 3:16: "For God so loved the world, that he gave his only begotten Son, that whosoever believeth in him should not perish, but have everlasting life."

I know God loved souls enough to send His Son, but I think this verse also points us to the fact that He loved the world—the beauty of nature itself—enough to send redemption to us who live in the world. And if He loves the world, He wants us to love it and enjoy it. When Adam and Eve were first created, God told them to have dominion over the earth. I'm sure that part of this instruction was for them to enjoy His handiwork including "every tree that is pleasant to the sight, and good for food" (Genesis 2:9). In 1 Timothy 6:17 Paul makes it clear that God "richly provides us with everything for our enjoyment" (NIV).

To get to my brother's home, I have to drive down Druid Lane. The lane is tree-lined; Spanish moss hangs down and waves lazily in the breeze. The road is named for the druids who lived in Ireland about the time of Christ. These people found such tranquility in nature they didn't much consider the God who created it.

In contrast to the druids, I think of the psalmist who obviously drank in the delights of nature—yet always seemed to remember that "the earth is the Lord's, and the fulness thereof; the world, and they that dwell therein" (Psalm 24:1), and that the Lord was the owner of "the cattle upon a thousand hills" (50:10).

The psalmist David also knew that God has arranged a perpetual performance through nature—for our therepeutic benefit. He's the one who said that the Lord "maketh me to lie down in green pastures" and "leadeth me beside the still waters" (23:2). He's the one who said, "I will lift up mine eyes unto the hills, from whence cometh my help" (121:1). David—a shepherd turned king—knew the importance of being tuned in to nature.

I've heard people say that after age forty it's just "paint, scrape, and patch." But the older and *wiser* I get, the more I see that it doesn't have to be that way—if I remember to be mindful of God's natural gifts to me, if I remember that He wants me to quit rushing and begin to appreciate the world's natural beauty.

Time and Space

I grew up in a parsonage. My dad preached against working on Sunday. He knew the commandments. "Six days thou shalt do thy work, and on the seventh day thou shalt rest" (Exodus 23:12).

Yet Sunday at our house was our busiest, hardest day of the week. Dad preached twice; Mother taught a Sunday school class; I taught a Sunday school class; my brothers and I were in the orchestra; we played an offertory, sang a family song, played loudly before the service, and played softly during the altar call; on Sunday afternoon we had a jail or nursing home service. After church on Sunday night we had company come over. Mother served either her homemade hamburgers complete with everything or her hot fudge sundaes that put Dairy Queen to shame.

We gave our all on Sunday, and Monday morning, we kids had a hard time getting up the steps of the orange school bus.

My dad always had a "hangover" on Monday—a headache and diarrhea. But after a few years he wised up and declared Monday a nature day. During the school year, he and Mother would relax outdoors or drive up to the hills near Rockville, Indiana, through the old covered bridges (which are still there), around the river bends. They'd walk through the leaves in the heavily wooded hills—picking mushrooms, sweet Williams, or jack-in-the-pulpits.

When school was out, the family took boat rides down the Wabash River, went swimming in the north gravel pit near Otter Creek, or worked in the garden. We picked wild strawberries along the railroad tracks or played with our pet animals.

We grew up with enough space to hit a baseball without breaking out windows. If we moved to a church that had a parsonage on a busy street, my dad would rent it out, take the money, and find us a place in the country. With four boys and a girl who loved animals, the city people were glad our family moved "out"!

Carl grew up in downtown Cleveland, Ohio, where the rain from the neighbors' roof merged with theirs in a *mutual* downspout. Yet his parents didn't deny their children the wonders of nature. They took Carl and his brother to Lake Erie every Saturday.

Have you ever noticed that even music gets its life from its rests and pauses? The sounds and notes cannot be constant and sustained; to be pleasant, tranquilizing, or even entertaining, they must be rhythmically planned with *rests*.

God knew what He was doing when He said we need a day of rest and Jesus made that clear when he said, "The sabbath was made for man, and not man for the sabbath" (Mark 2:27).

I've always kept Sunday apart as the Lord's Day, but, like my father, I seem to fill that day with service instead of with rest and relaxation.

Last spring amid hustle and activity of work, I decided that I needed a rest so I would be able to make "more beautiful music." I was born on Wednesday, so I decided to declare Wednesday "My Day." I don't take a whole day off, but a small part—a pit stop to get recharged for my week's journey. I decided to plan for My Day, look forward to it, and celebrate it.

Last Wednesday afternoon, I treated myself to a nap—the first afternoon nap I'd taken since I was in kindergarten. Boy, did it feel good.

But sometimes I don't follow through on my own plans or follow my own advice.

Months ago I wrote a note to a friend of mine, "I see you

147

rushing, hurrying your life. You were born six blocks from the Indy 500 racetrack, and you've been drag racing all your life. Slow down, enjoy your family and live."

This summer I received an envelope with her return address in the upper left corner. I opened it eagerly and was struck between the eyes with her reply. She had returned my note with a small P.S.: "I've been reading the papers; take your own advice."

She was right. I had been traveling, writing, working too much, too long, and I was wearing down.

About the same time my phone rang. I almost broke out in hives. *Should I answer it?* I wondered. *Will it be something else to do?*

I couldn't resist. I answered the phone and heard, "Hello, this is Deb Elhard." She quickly acknowledged that we were strangers. "But," she said, "one of my friends read your book *Super Natural Living* and thought you might be the only person around today who would like to go raspberry picking with me."

I dropped everything and met her at the door. She arrived wearing one of her husband's shirts, a pair of faded, soft, well-fitting jeans. She had no makeup on, a casual hairdo, a ready smile, and a spirit that was in tune with nature. How I enjoyed our conversation. We drove six miles out to Ewalt's farm where you can pick your own red raspberries, black raspberries, and —believe it or not—*gold* raspberries for $1 a box. At the end of the day my arms were so scratched I wondered if I needed a blood transfusion.

I was tired, but it was a "good" tired; I was back "in synch" with nature, with life. What a tonic that day—that new friend—was.

That wonderful memory has a postscript. The following evening Carl and I attended a theatre presentation in the city park. Our daughter Connie played the part of a country girl looking for a man, but I gasped with surprise when I saw that Deb Elhard was playing the role of the mother, a widowed bumpkin. She was a wonderful actress and I suspected she soaked in a great deal of her creative energy from that most effective booster shot— the great oudoors.

A Matter of Life or Death

Sometimes our slowing down and taking care of ourselves is not just a matter of refreshing our creativity or recharging our batteries. Sometimes tuning in to nature is a matter of life or death. Virginia Brazier, who gave me this little anonymous poem, knew exactly what I'm referring to:

> *"This is the age of the half-read page,*
> *And the quick hash, and the mad dash,*
> *The bright night, with the nerves tight,*
> *The plane hop, with the brief stop,*
> *The lamp tan, in a short span,*
> *The big shot, in a good spot,*
> *And the brain strain, and the heart pain,*
> *Til the spring snaps, and the fun's done."*

Our neighbor in North Dakota, Bill Van Garvin, is something of an expert with a bow and arrow. He's taught me a lesson or two on how he cares for it. He strings the bow tightly only when he is ready to shoot. When he returns home, he rests the bow string by loosening it so it will not sag or, worse, break from constant strain. The more I thought about it, the more I saw that bows are like people; we, also, can string ourselves too tightly for too long.

I know a young widow whose husband had been warned to

slow down. The surgeon at Gainesville Heart Center had told him, "If you slow down, work no more than six hours a day, you will live as long as anyone." But his widow later told me, "He refused to relax. He wanted things. He drove himself to prove his success to the family and our friends."

He told that doctor, "I would rather live half as long and twice as good." And he did.

I sat with another woman in a doctor's office. She had chronic tension from anxiety and worry, plus headaches, indigestion, and colitis. I heard the doctor tell her to quit making her house a showplace, to drink from six to eight glasses of water a day, and eat one-fourth cup of bran each morning or evening. Then I listened to her reply: "I don't use my house, it uses me. I hate the taste of bran, and water is bland."

Eight years later, I attended her funeral.

Too often we ask God for miracles, refuse to do our homework, and will not keep pace, in tune, with nature's rhythm.

Here are some specific ways we can benefit and grow from God's handiwork.

Let the Merry Sunshine In

For years children have loved to sing the "merry sunshine" song, especially in the morning when the sun breaks the night darkness with its scary shadows. But the truth of that song is probably lost on those young children who are oblivious to the fact that sunlight is very important to a person's well-being.

Of course green plants need the sunlight to grow and to produce fruit, but animals—and people?

April has a cat named Disco that risks her life every morning by stretching out and sleeping on the third step of our staircase.

Disco also puts the life of my family in jeopardy; anyone going up or coming down could trip on her since she is the same color as the carpet. We have chased her away and scolded her any number of times, yet she continues to sprawl out on the third step, because that's where she can bask in the morning sun.

Finally I bought a dumb book on the personality of cats. But I learned one interesting point, that God through nature teaches cats to extend the hairs of their fur to the solar rays of the sun. They absorb vitamin C and energy, so they can, nocturnal as they are, "cat around" at night.

I've also read that some psychiatrists, as part of a program of therapy to relieve depression, have patients sit outside in the direct rays of the sun with their eyes closed for twenty minutes a day. The thin skin of the eyelids and on the backs of their hands can then absorb solar rays and vitamin C. The researcher suggested that those who live in a cold climate should sit by a window for twenty minutes. Even women who are extremely busy could sit and write, sit and sew, or sit and type near a window to relieve depression.

I have a friend who was struggling through menopause. Her husband invited a psychiatrist home for dinner, and his advice was, "For your mind's sake, open the drapes, let the light in. Install lots of overhead fluorescent lighting." It worked. In two weeks my friend was more cheerful.

There is none so blind as she who closes her eyelids when there is a solution in sight. Sometimes we have to *do* something to fight depression. You act your way into feeling, not feel your way into acting. You have limited influence over your subconscious, but over your *conscious mind* you have *full control*. Sometimes we must open the drapes.

Recently I went to Miami to do a telecast. I drove six hours, from the west coast of Florida to the east, and arrived at the hotel tired. Exhausted, I carried my wrinkled clothes to my room so I could get ready to drive through the madhouse traffic to the studio. As soon as I walked in I said, "I'm not going to get along well on this trip. I'm not going to like it here." The room was dark, the drapes were pulled and the predominant color in the room was avocado green. Since I once saw my innards oozing gangrene after a ruptured appendix, that color turns me *off*. Then, when I heard a lot of masculine voices yelling, I thought things were going to be even worse. *Oh, no,* I thought, *this is not a motel, but a roughhouse.* Exasperated I jerked open the drapes. . . . What a surprise! I was on the eighth floor and the balcony opened onto an expanse of lake, palm trees, and a horse race in full progress. Now I have raised quarterhorses for thirty-six years, and have never seen such gorgeous horseflesh! It was stimulant to my adrenalin. I went to that television program pumped. But what if I hadn't opened the drapes. . . ?

Walk a Mile in Your Own Shoes

Sometimes (especially on Wednesdays) I walk alone, usually three to five miles right after breakfast or lunch. (This takes one hour and forty minutes.) I pray aloud, talk to God, think about my writing. I am amazed that when I breeze out the cobwebs of my mind in this way, I can return home and write an entire chapter in half the time it otherwise takes.

Walking sets the mind free. The mind is mysteriously oiled by the body's easy rhythm. The creative juices start flowing.

I'm not the only one who praises the virtues of walking. W. H. Davies said, " 'Shall I walk or shall I ride?' 'Ride,' pleasure said. 'Walk,' joy replied."

I'm sure Lewis Carroll had more than miles in mind when Alice in Wonderland said, "You will get somewhere if you walk long enough."

Here in Florida, I've met Toni Morrow, director of activities at the renowned resort Innisbrook. Toni reintroduced Carl and me to the "perfect" exercises, walking, swimming, bicycle-riding, reminding us that most doctors recommend walking.

Toni explained to me that thousands of people drive south to Florida to enjoy a break from winter. But they shelf up in high-rise condos or pack into layered motels.

They then need a break from all the noisy neighbors. She orchestrates cruises and plans exotic entertainment, but she says the greatest therapeutic benefits of that retreat are enjoyed on the paths that wind through twelve hundred acres of trees, bushes, creeks, and flowering gardens. Each spring they plant a hundred new trees so the foliage need never wane.

They do a great service to people who need the open spaces, but sometimes our spirits can draw in even more strength from walking where nature has not been rearranged by the hand of man. My neighbor across the pond in Sisseton, Sandy Anderson, had a "back forty" meadow covered with black-eyed Susans. From a prairie woman she had learned that they most likely grow and bloom in virgin soil that has never been plowed and in grass that has never been mowed. I loved to walk in that field and experience the cure of fearful worry. I could clear my mental computer and think about nothing at all.

The closer I get to undefiled nature, the more apt I am to try to visualize the Garden of Eden, where Adam and Eve walked and talked with God. In the garden there was no artificial noise, no need for splashy entertainment. Adam and Eve saw the sky, looked at each other, the flowers and trees. They listened to each other, to the mockingbird, the nightingale. Eve was not just a "sleeping bag" but a mate who walked through nature with her mate—and together they talked with God. As I see it, nature was their mother and God, their father. Didn't God form Adam from the soil of the earth?

I like to walk alone—just my God and me—but a walking companion—especially Carl—can add an extra element of pleasure. A good walking partner gives solitude and company at the same time. The sense of solitude allows your imagination to be revived and the companionship helps keep you centered in reality.

Smell the Roses

One afternoon I witnessed a quarrel between two friends. What I heard tore me apart. I was pulled by both sides between loyalty and truth. Later when I was alone, I put on my lightweight Brooks walking shoes and took off, walking fast past the Dickey County fairgrounds, just east of Highway 281 in Ellendale, down a gravel road, past acres of sunflower fields in full bloom—a million yellow flower faces turned in the same direction, toward the brightest sunlight. That sight was a tonic to my eyes, a therapy to my anxious mind.

I kept walking vigorously, but then suddenly stopped short. Not twelve feet away were two tiny flickertail deer, noses twitching, tails held high feeling the wind on their flanks. When I started whispering to them, walking toward them, they turned slowly and walked at my pace, a little in front. In a minute they bolted, leaping a six-foot fence and dashing down between straight rows of young tender corn.

I kept walking to ease yet more tension and not ten minutes

later I looked to the right and there, standing on a foothill of green pasture grass, were a mare and a contentedly nursing colt. The mother's head drooped in the warm sun, eyes closed, enjoying her loving, nourishing task.

A farmer bailing hay nearby had stopped to watch the same sight. He had turned off the motor of his tractor and he leaned back against a stack of hay and munched a yellow apple. About the time I saw him I was startled by a wonderful aroma. It had been a long while since I had taken time to inhale the fragrance of newly mown hay. It was so wonderful, it outshone all the sights of the day. And in the wonder of that experience I finally felt the tension and hurt drift away from me, and I was able to get the perspective I needed on that troubling situation. I've thought about that encounter with nature many times and marveled at this God-given sense of smell. Your eyes can fool you; your mind will lie; even sounds can deceive; but smells always tell the truth. It is in the smell that memory is lodged. As Andrei Codrescu said, "The smells of childhood are the road maps of the past."

As you smell, as you inhale deeply, you can "winterize" or "summerize" your life. You can enjoy the full keyboard of spring, fall, summer, and winter just through God's wonderful gift of smell.

Our daughter Carol lives in Vail, Colorado. She says her soul stays toned up not just by the thrill of action—flying downslope on skis—but by the smell of the frost and the life that is in the hillside air.

What are some of my favorite smells? The smell of peanut butter fudge cooking on the stove. The smell of horse stables in Texas. The ocean at low tide. The smell of the third-floor attic room in our old house in North Dakota—my writing hideaway.

The significance of smell is greater than just our physical

responsiveness. There are spiritual analogies as well. As the song says, we are missing out on life if we don't take the time to stop and smell the roses. James 1:17 says, "Every good gift and every perfect gift is from above, and cometh down from the Father of lights." I can't help but think that the gift of smell is one of the little extra gifts that God, in His creative genius, added in for us to enjoy as we tune in to His wonderful world.

In 2 Corinthians 2:15, the apostle Paul uses our sense of smell in an unusual metaphor. He says that we Christians are "the aroma of Christ"—or at least we should be. There's an old Gospel song that's based on Song of Solomon 2:1. It says that Jesus is "the lily of the valleys." That Bible verse also says, "I am the rose of Sharon." What wonderful images to illustrate how rich and aromatic God wants us to be.

Take a Mini-Vacation

I remember one morning when I was particularly harried. The phone would not stop ringing; the mail was stacked up; I bumped my head rounding the corner to answer the doorbell. When I finally stopped to catch a breath I realized that my fists were clenched tightly and I was biting my lips. I had read Matthew 11:28: "Come unto me, all ye that labor and are heavy laden, and I will give you rest. . . . Learn of me . . . and ye shall find rest unto your souls"; I had read Isaiah 11:10: "His rest shall be glorious"; I'd even read Isaiah 28:12: "This is the rest wherewith ye may cause the weary to rest; and this is the refreshing," but just reading the words wasn't enough.

I was hot, sweaty, and uptight, and I knew what I needed to do was to get back in tune with life—I had to get in tune with God's nature. It was ten minutes until lunchtime, and I left my

156

husband a quick note: "Dear Adam, eat at the school cafeteria. I've gone out for lunch. See you this P.M." I signed it, "Love, Eve."

I didn't head for a restaurant. Rather, I quickly threw the following into a brown sack: one package of almonds, one mini-box of raisins, one carrot, one celery stick, a yellow apple, and two slices of sharp cheese. I was afraid that if I took time to wrap each item separately in plastic someone would come by or call and prevent my escape. The brown sack went into my bicycle basket and I rode out past the fairgrounds to a rickety bridge, where I stopped and munched my lunch. I had no napkin. I even drank water from the creek with my hands. But the trip was successful. When I returned I was ready to tackle life again. Don't get me wrong, I love to be domestic, bake, socialize, but I must "intermission" to survive.

Anyone can take minute vacations between dashes. Try taking the phone off the hook at 8:00 A.M. or 8:00 P.M. so you can soak in a tub and enjoy the refreshing feel of the warm water; imagine yourself floating in the Caribbean. Put on your swimsuit and lie on a towel draped over the cellar door; soak up the sun like Disco the cat. Ride your bike through the cemetery and thank God you're not rushing to your death. Walk to the post office. Bake an apple pie and enjoy the aroma. You don't have to spend money to go to the Bahamas. You can vacation any time of the day.

God is the author of creation and has recreation at hand—if you are in tune with nature.

10

Increase the Mirth Rate

"He that is of a merry heart hath a continual feast."

Proverbs 15:15

It was almost midnight when I arrived in town for a TV appearance the next morning. I wanted to get right to the hotel to get to bed but, you guessed it, the airline had lost my luggage.

I had to take the time to fill out a claim and the man who worked with me said, "I'm doing a survey on personality and humor—how the religious people who come through here react to lost luggage."

Interesting, I thought. Now I wish I'd asked him what he'd found out but at the time humor wasn't the topic of a chapter of a book I was writing. I simply told him my honest reaction to the loss. "It will be here before the telecast in the morning," I said with great assurance.

He'd obviously been working for an airline company for quite some time. "And if it isn't . . . ?" he asked.

Well, it wasn't, and as I got ready to go to the studio the next morning I knew I had a choice. The clothes I had on were old, casual, and comfortable, perfect for traveling but inappropriate for a television appearance. I could wear them in defeat or I could take the "joke" on the chin.

I started the interview by suggesting that we sing, "Just As I Am," explaining, "If I look like I've slept in my clothes, it's because I did."

I hoped the airline employee who was taking the survey was watching the interview that morning. I wanted him to see that Christians can see the light side of life, even if it involves disappointment or things not turning out as we'd planned.

A Good Medicine

There are many Bible verses about laughter, mirth, and joy, but Proverbs 17:22 is probably the most familiar: "A merry heart doeth good like a medicine: but a broken spirit drieth the bones."

I may be accused of mixing metaphors, but I can't imagine anything more "out of tune" with life than dry bones. Ezekiel had a vision in which he saw a whole valley strewn with bones that were "very dead and very dry." But they didn't stay that way. As Ezekiel watched, God restored life to those bones. They were connected together, covered with muscles and sinews and skin and those dry bones finally stood before Ezekiel as "an exceeding great army" (Ezekiel 37:10).

In a mysterious way laughter does "good like a medicine." I received a letter from "Mrs. B.," a registered nurse who works at a medical center in Springfield, Missouri. She heard that I was doing a chapter on mirth and she wanted to share a dramatic story that showed the value of humor. In medical training nurses and aides are alerted to be careful about what they say in front of patients, even if they are unconscious. Though people may appear to be unresponsive to the environment, they can often hear bedside conversations. One day Mrs. B. and a younger student nurse were routinely checking on a thirteen-year-old boy who had been comatose for eight weeks.

The younger nurse, who had been dying to get Mrs. B. alone to tell her about a ridiculously funny blunder made by Dr. M., couldn't wait a minute longer. She blurted the story in the presence of the patient. The two women roared with laughter, and then stopped short. They heard a muffled hum, and noticed that the boy's abdomen was vibrating. He was trying to get a laugh out. For several minutes they stood and watched him; as they continued talking, he stirred and opened his eyes to the world. Four days later he went home! He said that their merry laughter had seemed to wake him up from a nightmare from which he hadn't been able to shake loose.

Medical science is becoming increasingly aware of the health benefits of laughter. (They are verifying what Solomon, the wisest man ever to live, already told us.)

Last Christmas several family members got together. As Aunt Gwen was leaving she fell and rolled head over heels down a flight of sixteen stairs. It knocked her out, and broke a picture frame she was carrying so that she was badly cut by the glass. When she came to, she looked up into our frightened faces and apologized to Carl, "I'm sorry I scared everyone when I fell. The next time I'll slide down the bannister." I'm sorry to say she also hurt her hip and spent several days in the hospital. But the doctor attributed her rapid recovery to her attitude and sense of humor.

She joked, "Why worry? You can get gray hair from worrying about your teeth falling out."

Doctors reassure us that there are three safety valves that prevent mental illness, even insanity. They are tears, music, and humor/laughter.

Dr. William Fry of Stanford University Medical School says, "Laughter works by stimulating the brain to produce hormones that help ease pain. It also stimulates the endocrine system which may relieve symptoms of disease. Laughter can help ease feelings of depression."

Given the research about humor and health, can we afford not to laugh?

At Home, At Work, At Play

While I was working at Central Bible College, at Trinity College, and here in Florida with retired people, I took a poll. I asked several hundred people to rate six qualities they would look for if they were selecting a new marriage partner: (1) sense of humor, (2) looks, (3) size, (4) age, (5) money, (6) religion. More than ninety percent put *sense of humor* at the top of their list.

That informal survey says it all: Laughter is a prime ingredient of a successful marriage, even more than religion. In fact, unfortunately, our religious faith often is the lid that squelches a light spirit.

My husband, in his counseling experience, has been saddened over and over again by this scenario: a successful man leaves a demanding, super-religious wife and runs off with an "airhead," simply because life got too heavy. The "new woman" was light-hearted, knew how to laugh, could relax with him. On the other side of the coin, I've seen older women leave their families and run off to California to meet up with bronze-bodied beach bums. Why? Because their husbands' condescension and self-righteousness squelched their ability to laugh.

If we are wise, we will ask God to help us help each other bloom.

Humor is also valuable to our children. Psalm 16:6 says, "The boundary lines have fallen for me in pleasant places; surely I have a delightful inheritance" (NIV). I love this verse because it's been so true for me. My mother was a one-woman entertainment center. Our family survived the great Depression, a dozen parsonages, poverty, misunderstanding, and my four brothers because of her great sense of humor. She could roll with the punches, cope with disappointment, and rebound. She taught us to look for humor to follow embarrassment—just as surely as day follows night. When I think of the "delightful inheritance" she gave to me, I think of her finely tuned sense of humor. I only hope I can pass it on to her grandchildren—even in my ability to laugh at the simple absurdities of modern American culture: the traverse rod box with fine print, "Some assembly required"; the dotted lines indicating where the pouring spout is on the box of powdered milk; the plastic garbage bag that splits before you can get it to the curb. Have you ever tried to open those little bags of peanuts you get in an airplane? It takes a hacksaw to get them open—as well as some of the new childproof, spillproof pill bottles.

Jackie Ransdell shared with me the following short piece she wrote, entitled "The Special Mother."

*   *   *

Somehow I visualize God hovering over earth selecting His instruments for propagation with great care and deliberation. As He observes, He instructs His angels to take notes in a giant ledger.

"Armstrong, Beth, a son. Patron saint, Matthew.

"Forest, Marjorie, daughter. Patron, saint, Cecilia.

"Rutledge, Carrie, twins. Patron saint . . . give her Gerard, he's used to profanity."

Finally, He passes a name to an angel and smiles. "Give her a handicapped child."

The angel is curious. "Why this one, God? She's so happy."

"Exactly. Could I give a handicapped child a mother who doesn't know laughter? That would be cruel."

"But does she have patience?" asks the angel.

"I don't want her to have too much patience, or she'll drown in a sea of self-pity and despair. Once the shock and resentment wear off, she'll handle it.

"I watched her today. She has a sense of self and independence so rare and so necessary in a mother. You see, the child I'm going to give her has his own world. She has to make it live in her world, and that's not going to be easy."

"But Lord, I don't think she even believes in You."

God smiles. "No matter, I can fix that. This one is perfect. She has just enough selfishness."

The angel gasps. "Selfishness? Is that a virtue?"

"Well, if she can't separate herself from the child occasionally, she'll never survive. Yes, here is a woman whom I will bless with a child less than perfect. She doesn't realize it yet, but she is to be envied.

"She will never take for granted a spoken word. She will never consider a step ordinary. When her child says 'Momma' for the first time, she will be witness to a miracle and know it. When she describes a tree or a sunset to her blind child, she will see it as few people ever see my creations.

"I will permit her to see clearly the things I see—ignorance, cruelty, prejudice—and allow her to rise above them.

"She will never be alone. I will be at her side every minute of every day of her life because she is doing My work as surely as she is here by My side."

"And what about her patron saint?" asks the angel, his pen poised in mid-air.

God smiles. "A mirror will suffice."

Anyone's work environment can also benefit from a little levity. I have found that women are rarely good at anything they don't have a little fun doing. Yet current statistics on the American job place are disturbing: Only twenty percent of workers like what they do. A few laughs during the day may improve that percentage and the quality of our work. Studies show that for managers, a sense of humor is important. It creates rapport and reduces conflict and relieves stress.

Susan RoAne is a lecturer on career marketing strategies. A magazine, *Executive Female*, has featured her, praising her for her practical representations and dynamic sense of humor. Susan has done some research on women and humor, and she concludes that a sense of humor is a survivor tool for women in business.

At the Tampa airport I met a taxi driver who was hoping a laugh would help make for loyal customers. He drove me to my destination and as I got out I tipped him generously. He thanked me, then gave me his card which said, "Please call me again." But that's not all. I burst out laughing at the clever message:

IMPORTANT TELEPHONE NUMBERS

Ronald Reagan 202-456-1414
President of the U.S.A.

John Paul II 00396/69 82
The Pope

M. Gorbachev 007-095-205-25 11
Sec. C.C. of the KPdSU
Moscow Red Square 4

Dr. Helmut Kohl 0228/561
Federal Chancellor
W. Germany

Elizabeth II 00441/930-48 32
Queen of the United Kingdom

Shimon Peres 009722/55 41 11
Prime Minister, Israel

Woody's Taxi Service 784-3000
Woody Turner, Proprietor

His touch of humor surely made the trip memorable, and that pleasant memory might very well prompt people to give him a call.

Sugar-Coated Messages

Laughter is God's hand on the shoulder of a troubled world. I think God designed us so we could laugh and thereby release a lot of tension that could otherwise creep into our relationships—any of our relationships.

A word fitly spoken in humor can remove pain and promote forgiveness. Recently Carl and I were discussing a delicate issue and suddenly he shot an arrow in my direction. It hit the mark and it stung for several days. I felt his remark was unfair since he spoke quickly without knowing all the details of the circumstance. He didn't repent on bended knee with sackcloth and ashes, but two days later in the mail I got a card. A large face covered the entire front panel and a large Band-Aid covered the entire mouth. Inside one word was printed in small letters: "sorry." How can you stay mad at a guy with that kind of humor?

Words of humor can also be gentle, subtle reprimands, as the laughter lowers a person's defensiveness. If you—the one finding fault—are smiling, he—the "offending" party—can usually receive your comments without being overburdened with guilt. The smile softens the message.

I got a cartoon from a friend to whom I had owed a letter for a long time. It showed Snoopy looking into an empty mailbox with the caption, "An empty mailbox echoes so loudly!"

If I want to coach my children I often write a note such as this one I taped up in the kitchen: "If you insist on eating breakfast standing up, splattering jelly on the floor, please stand over the kitchen sink. I don't mind cleaning the sink, but I won't stoop to the floor." I signed it, "The Management." Or late at night: "Self-cleaning kitchen: Clean up after your*self*. Betty's off duty."

I know a man who bought his wife two bumper stickers, hoping she'd get a message about one of her weaknesses. One slogan was: "Shop Till You Drop." The other sticker said, "A Woman's Place Is in the Mall." The subtle humor was amazingly effective.

Humor is an excellent way for a minister to get his message home without offending. The youth pastor at Trinity College is a master at this prodding humor. When he wants to get a message

across to the faculty children he does it with humor, and it works.
I have his permission to pass one on to you:

THE LOVE CHAPTER (NYV)
(New Youth Version)
by Jeffery Nelson

Though I sing as an angel and getteth first at National
Teen Talent, and have not love, I am become as static on
the radio or a squealing hearing aid. And though I have the
gift of quizzing and understand all chapters and though I
memorize entire books, so that I could quote passages
fluently, and have not love, I am wasted. And though I
bestow all my albums and tapes to the poor, and though I
collect rock records to be burned, and have not love, I am
a nerd.

Love is patient with little brothers and sisters, and is kind
even to the jerks, love does not jealously want Joe Cool's
Camaro or Suzie's 501 Levis, love does not step on others
to get higher, is not big headed. Doth not show off to
impress a date, isn't looking out for "Number One," and is
not easily ticked off, reflecteth on no evil thought, rejoiceth
not in gossip, but sticketh up for the truth. Putteth up with
all things, diggeth all good things, encourageth in all
things, tolerateth all things.

Love never faileth: but whether there be Teen Talent, it
shall fail; whether there be quizzes, they shall cease;
whether there be dramatic productions, they shall vanish
away. For we know our drama parts and we sing our youth
choir parts, but when that which is perfect is come, then
that which is in parts shall be done away.

When I was an elementary twerp, I spake as a twerp, I understood as a twerp, I thought as a twerp; but when I became a high schooler, I put away twerpish things.

For now we see the game from the bleachers, but then we will be right on the court, then I will know even as the coach knoweth. And now abideth faith, hope, love, these three; and if love isn't the greatest then gaggeth me with a spooneth.

I've lived with enough teenagers that I could "Amen" his paraphrase—even as I cracked a smile.

Taking Yourself Out of the Heat

Elsa Maxwell's father gave her a delightful inheritance, just as my mother passed one on to me. Just before he died he told her: (1) Never collect inanimate objects, (2) Don't worry about *they*, and (3) Laugh at yourself before others have a chance to laugh at you.

We can save ourselves from a lot of pain if we are able to learn to laugh at ourselves when we are in an embarrassing situation.

Some time ago I was attending an out-of-town softball tournament in which April was playing. Our team didn't have many spectators. I was one of a few parents who had driven to Jamestown to cheer the team on. I must say I was doing a good job. If an enthusiastic mother could have made any difference I think we would have won by that alone. The kids were pleased I had come along, and to show appreciation, one of the second-string players bought me a Slow Poke, a caramel sucker—giant-sized. I licked at it, sucked on it, then decided to bite off the end. What a mistake. The front jacket cap of my tooth snapped, fell out of my mouth, and down between the bleachers into a sea of dirt-covered popcorn. I was horrified. Why me? Why here? Why now? I *had* to find it, so I scrambled down under the bleachers and combed the popcorn, praying no one would see me. As the Bible says, seek and ye shall find—and I did. I sneaked back to my seat and for the rest of the inning, I held that cap tightly in my fist.

Suddenly you'd have thought I was in a Quaker meeting: "No more laughing, no more talking, no more having fun"—well, at least no more cheering on.

Once April looked up and with her eyes and lips said, "What's wrong?" I merely smiled—with my mouth open—and she knew. She looked like she would faint, then broke into laughter. At that point, I retreated to the car in the parking lot and waited out the game, which our team was winning. The kids had planned a celebration meal for us "faithful" parents. I hated to miss such an event, but my pride was winning—until my ingenuity got the upper hand. As I sat in the car I got a great idea. I chewed a small bit of chewing gum until it was soft. I poked it in the hole in my gum and shoved the tooth in place. It held! I thought I was a genius. I'd just have to be unusually quiet the rest of the day. . . .

When we got to Bonanza, most ordered steak. I knew that wouldn't work. It was a cool day, I remarked, and a bowl of hot soup would taste good to me.

Oops. I'd run out of good ideas. I might as well have ordered steak. After only a few sips the chewing gum melted. The tooth plopped into my bowl and my secret was out.

At this point, I had a choice: I could go to the car and pout or I could swallow my pride and laugh.

The rest of the evening was great fun—at my expense. On the

way home April said, "Mother, that was a great performance! Few women could have handled such an embarrassment that well."

Embarrassing situations often occur when we just don't manage to "fix things up" to fit the mold society has for us. In some cultures nobody gives a second thought to lost teeth.

The secret of laughing at yourself is giving yourself freedom to slip out of the rigid roles when necessary—accepting them for what they are (societal expectations) and yourself for what you are (human and fallible).

When I visited South Africa I learned a lot about cultural roles and rules. And there the best jokes were on me.

A woman named Gillian met me at the Johannesburg airport and led me to her car in the parking lot. We loaded my bags and I headed for the right front seat. Being a gracious hostess, Gillian quietly asked, "Does Madame wish to drive?" I'd not even considered the possibility that South Africans would drive like the English—with the steering wheel on the right instead of the left. Then as she drove out of the airport, I suddenly panicked when I saw a large semi truck heading toward us, driving down the wrong side of the road. Some automatic reflex from my forty years of driving experience took over. I grabbed at the wheel and prepared to die. Gill, however, kept her cool and sweetly explained to me that she was not driving on the *wrong* side of the road, but the *left* side.

A few minutes later I again held on tight when a dial on the dashboard said—I thought—that we were going 120, then 130 miles per hour. Wrong again. They were not miles per hour, but kilometers per hour.

I never did get acclimated to their traffic direction. I almost got killed crossing the street in Port Elizabeth. My friend Ruth

Nortje saved my life by grabbing the back of my dress and pulling hard.

When we can laugh at ourselves we are sending a message to those around us: I'm comfortable with who I am and I want you to be comfortable, too.

I think it is great when specific population groups can tell jokes on themselves. No one can tell "Texan" jokes like someone who's always lived there. They tell great "Aggie" jokes. No one can tell "Sister" jokes like a nun. Recently I heard a great "charismatic" joke: A Prebyterian died and walked up to heaven's gate. St. Peter greeted him and said, "It's easy to get in here, just spell *God.*" The Presbyterian spelled the word and St. Peter opened the gate and let him walk through. Then a Methodist died and he asked St. Peter, "Is it easy to enter here?" St. Peter said, "Yep. All you have to do is spell *God.*" He spelled it, G-O-D, and walked right in. Then a charismatic died. He arrived at the gate and asked, "St. Peter, is it really true? Is it easy to get into heaven?" St. Peter answered, "That's right. There is no prejudice up here. All you have to do is spell *Albuquerque.*"

Not Now . . . Later

Sometimes our discomfort or embarrassment is so intense we can laugh only after the incident. In this case humor is "embarrassment past-tense" or "tragedy overcome."

As Jesus said in John 16:20: "Your sorrow shall be turned into joy."

I had driven three hours with my friend Gloria Hutchens to speak at Sauk Center, Minnesota, for a Saturday night church rally. It was November sixth, my birthday. We arrived there only ten minutes before I was to be introduced. While she went and told the pastor we had made it, I went downstairs to the restroom. As usual, the ladies' room was full and eighteen or twenty women were waiting in the hallway. The men's room was empty. I figured I'd temporarily claim the territory, so I slipped in and locked the door behind me. No one had seen me and no one would ever know.

Well, they had recently remodeled the restroom and had covered the cement steps that led up to the "white throne" with a very slick gray porcelain-finish paint. Although I stepped carefully, I whacked my head on the overhead plumbing. I winced and felt a painful knot on my head but I knew I would be all right. But when I started up the steps, my high wooden heels slipped. My feet went out from under me and I cracked the back of my head on that cement. When I woke up I was at the bottom of the steps. My back now hurt more than my head and my belt was broken. I could hear the congregation singing upstairs. I could not see my feet, and soon realized that the heels of my shoes had run hard through a plasterboard wall and were protruding into the hallway in the dust of white chalky powder.

I heard two men talking in the hall. One said, "What is this?" The other opened the door and answered, "I believe it's our speaker." "Not anymore," the first one remarked. "She'll never make it. She may be a writer, but she can't read." Then he called out and asked, "Do you know you're in the men's room?" "Yes," I muttered, although I didn't see what difference that made at this point in the game. Then came the second dumb question. "Are you hurt?" I couldn't help but reply, "No, I'm not hurt. I always exit the restroom this way."

I was determined I was going to speak. I assured them I would be okay, put my broken belt in my purse, and struggled to the platform. Somehow I got through the evening, but the pastor could tell that something was wrong. After church when I told him my story he wouldn't believe me until he'd gone to check it out for himself. Then—you should have heard the roar.

All the way home that night I moaned. I couldn't sleep and the next day the doctor told me I'd broken my tailbone—snapped off the last three tiny bones at the end of my spine. I didn't even try to explain the accident to the doctor. . . . Weeks later I got a letter from the pastor's secretary telling me they did not repair the hole, but posted a sign that says, "Betty Malz was here."

Looking back now the whole story is hilariously funny, and I can laugh. But, as the psalmist said, I had to endure the night of weeping before I was able to experience the joy of the morning.

In time my daughter Brenda was able to tune out some painful stereotyping correspondence and let her scraped ego be healed by laughter.

She is the one of the busiest young mothers you'll ever meet. One of her daughter's teachers once sent home a letter, "Dear Mrs. Smart, Since you don't work, would you be able to make and bring to school the following items. . . ."

Now, Brenda cooks, sews, does her own wallpapering and interior decorating; she mows the lawn, types research papers for her husband, and teaches private piano lessons to eight advanced students. She is a Brownie troop leader and volunteers at the church. She *does* work.

Another organization repeatedly sent her form letters: If there is an *asterisk* by your name, please be notified that you have been selected to help with. . . .

At first Brenda—and I—were angry. But now we joke about it. I even start my letters to her: "Dear Asterisk."

I've had some good laughs with a neighbor over what I'll call "The laundry soap incident." At first, the situation wasn't funny. My neighbor's husband owns a service station and he got a rash that he feared was syphilis—contracted from the toilets at work. He went to the doctor who took one look and said, "Does your wife have a complete set of drinking glasses yet?"

He'd seen the signs before; a slew of men had come in suffering because their wives had washed their shorts with a cheap brand of soap powder because they could get a free drinking glass tucked inside each box of that particular brand.

As I said, it wasn't funny at first—only after the fact, when he found out that one of his employees suffered the same "laundry soap" ailment. So much for trying to get something for nothing.

A Time to Cool It

Not all humor is funny. Laughing at ourselves is one thing, poking fun at other people—at their expense—is quite another. A sense of humor and practical jokes are not the same.

Sometimes it's easy to get caught up in a group that is "taking on" one person. Because we're part of a group, we feel safety in numbers and say things we later regret.

When April was in high school she not only played softball; she played basketball. Again, I was there, sitting on bleachers, rooting for her team. At one particular game it seemed very obvious to me—and to others—that the referee was making some bad calls, and always against our team. There were two American Indians on our team, and I suspected that this guy was prejudiced against them.

My cheering, I'm afraid, started to get personal. I called the referee the Pillsbury Dough Boy. I turned to another mother and said, "Will you hold him if I poke his fat stomach with my finger?" Of course I said this loud enough to get a lot of laughs.

Carl leaned over and told me to turn the volume down and quit pointing my comments at the referee. He was afraid they'd call a technical on me, and he said that if I wasn't careful the referee would come find me after the game.

Sure enough, as soon as the game was over, the man bounded up the bleachers two rows at a time. My heart started to race. I gave Carl one of those "What do I do now?" looks. He smiled one of those "You're on your own" smiles—until the referee burst into a grin, shoved his hand into mine, and said, "Mrs. Malz, I saw you up here. I've read all your books and I've seen you on 'The 700 Club.' I'm so glad to meet you in person."

Right then and there I was cured. Now, I am more careful about who I call what—especially when I'm in a crowd. My witness is like a candle set on a hill because, as a Christian, I bear Christ's name. What people see in me—or in you—they quickly attribute to Christ. And that awareness keeps me on my toes, even—or especially—in the humor department.

A God Who Laughs

Yet even if I slip up, I've learned that God Himself has a sense of humor. He has a mysterious way of working good out of the most unlikely situations. The Lord spoke to Isaiah and pointedly said, "My thoughts are not your thoughts, neither are your ways my ways. . . . As the heavens are higher than the earth, so are my ways higher than your ways and my thoughts than your thoughts" (55:8–9, NIV).

His "higher ways" are sometimes out of tune with my own sense of humor. I was horrified several years ago when I saw the cover of a special mass market paperback of my book *My Glimpse of Eternity*. I had thought the idea of it was great—an edition inexpensive enough for servicemen and truckers to pick up and buy. But the California publisher had put a nude woman on the front. It wasn't a vulgar pose—the back of a lean woman standing in a mist, looking at a rainbow. It was too late to protest. Twenty-five thousand copies had been printed.

I must admit there was something ingenius about the promotion. They had taken a phrase I had used in the story, "I stood as though I was naked before God, no pretense, no pride, alone facing death," and they'd gone on from there.

But what did God do with this edition that had just sickened me? Two weeks after it came out I got a call from a trucker. He said, "I did two things, no three, that I've never done before: I've never read a *whole* book, not even in school. But I read yours. I saw the naked woman on the front and thought *This is going to be good*. Two chapters later, I had a good case of 'Jesus' and, for the first time in my life, I prayed. Then last Sunday I went to church with my wife the first time in twenty-two years."

Now there's God's sense of humor! When I saw how God had used that cover to get His message through to this man I had to stand back and smile at His mysterious ways.

As George MacDonald said, "It is the Heart that is not yet sure of its God that is afraid to laugh in His presence."

The Joy of the Lord

Nehemiah 8:10 says that "the joy of the Lord is your strength." Barbara Johnson knows how true this is. She has built an entire national outreach, "Spatula Ministries," because people need to see that disappointment can be tempered by humor. Barbara's own experience was her proving ground. Multiple tragedies struck her home all about the same time. Her husband lay in a hospital for two years; one son was killed in Vietnam; another son son was killed in an auto accident. Her third son, a homosexual, left home. She says her mind went. She orbited to the ceiling, stuck there, and felt as if they would have to take a spatula to scrape her down. For two years, her lifeline was praying, gravitating toward happy people, talking on the phone, reading, and waiting. Eventually her husband recovered and her son was delivered from a prison of deception and perversion.

She and her husband have founded "Spatula Ministry" to support parents who have been disappointed with their children. She publishes one of the most delightful monthly papers I've ever seen—full of joy and laughter. Her prayer force is effective, and her two books have helped countless suffering couples cope with disappointment: *Where Does a Mother Go to Resign?* and *Fresh Elastic for Stretched Out Moms.* (See appendix.)

As Barbara learned, as I've learned, joy and laughter do come if we open ourselves to them, if we look beyond ourselves to the delights God sets before us.

Stop for a quick moment and think over the last seven days of your life. Have you laughed? If not, have you smiled? What was it that opened up those positive emotions?

Think about the next week and work to place yourself in opportunities that will bring a little humor into your life.

Has it been a long time since you've laughed with your husband or your children? Churn up your memory bank and reminisce about an incident that you're sure will bring a smile.

I have a friend who clips and saves funny lines or stories. Of course she laughs over them herself but she shares the joy. She slips them into letters and birthday cards so someone else's day will include an extra chuckle. Now there's a woman who is in tune with humor; she's always ready to pass it on.

Isaiah 35:10: "And the ransomed of the Lord shall return, and come to Zion with songs and everlasting joy upon their heads: they shall obtain joy and gladness, and sorrow and sighing shall flee away."

11

Survival! (In Tune with Simplicity)

"The Lord preserveth the simple."

Psalm 116:6

I'm a survivor. I was born into a skinny economy at the end of the great Depression, November 6, 1929. Although my father was a pastor, somehow our family survived, even thrived, while he pioneered nine small churches in Indiana. I experienced diptheria, a tornado in Indiana, a hurricane and sink hole in Florida, was thrown from a running horse, had surgery on my voice box removing five nodes, and had an English walnut-sized tumor removed from down inside my spinal column. I survived a ruptured appendix for eleven days with peritonitis (gangrene), pneumonia, three surgeries, was in a coma unconscious for forty-four days and died for twenty-eight minutes. Two years later, my husband died following open heart surgery, leaving me pregnant with our second baby. She was born four months after his death. I survived on Social Security for six years with two small daughters, then married a returned missionary with three

179

children whose wife had died with cancer. When I said, "I do," at the altar, I became a bride, a pastor's wife, a stepmother, a mother-in-law, a grandmother, and now my initials are B.M.! I believe that I qualify as a survivor.

I have learned through these storms of life to cope with disappointment, roll with the punches, to rebound and bounce back and to pray, pray, pray. If I can suggest a shortcut, relieve someone from making some of the mistakes I made, or add a little zest to your life, I want to pass on some personal tips.

Imagine yourself afloat on the sea of life. Your life raft, I have learned, must be equally inflated in five compartments with: Good health, good relationships, a sense of humor, prayer and simplicity.

Life is like a sandwich. You cannot arrive here without God. He gives that first initial breath when the doctor cuts the birth cord. You cannot get out of this life without facing God, choosing life or death, eternal heaven or hell. (These are the top and bottom bun of the sandwich.) If you recognize Him early at the beginning and long for Him at the end, He fills the center of your life with the "good meat," real living!

Each day is like an Oreo cookie. If you begin it with prayer and end it with prayer, He fills the day with that sweet, cream center all day long.

Health: Do your homework. God does the miraculous. Jesus heals, but you must breathe deep, sleep cool, eat light, exercise, drink lots of water, and control your weight to "prosper and be in health as your soul prospers." God is the Creator, but He won't mop your kitchen, spank the kids, cook, or love your husband for you. These are your jobs.

Good relationships: We become someone in relationship to

180

other people. We are a wife, a mother, an employee, a friend, a neighbor, even a child of God because of our relationships.

Sense of humor: The last thing a man needs at the end of a long day is a weepy woman. The last thing a woman needs at the end of a long day is a referee too busy calling fouls to play the game. Laugh at yourself. I was born a preemie at seven months. I came into this world badly wrinkled, and it looks like I'm going to go out the same way.

Prayer: Begin your A.M. quietly "absorbing Him." End your P.M. breathing His name, Jesus, silently, your benediction before falling into peaceful sleep.

Simplicity: From where I sit, this is the key to survival! Probably the first song that comes to mind when you mention simplicity is "Jesus loves me, this I know, for the Bible tells me so." The person who had the greatest Christian impact on your life was probably not a woman who roared and tooted loudly, but one who contained quiet power at the center of her being.

Simplicity is not always easy to attain. Simplicity perhaps is the most complicated of accomplishments.

If life has become complicated for you, that is *not* the work of God. In 2 Corinthians 11:3 Paul warns Christians of Satan's tactics: "I fear, lest by any means, as the serpent beguiled Eve through his subtilty, so your minds should be corrupted from the simplicity that is in Christ."

Jesus came to make life simple. He never hurried, never worried. He lived with the answer; He was the answer. Jesus was simply profound because He was so profoundly simple. His sermons were not heavy theological dissertations, but practical parables that even children could follow.

Jesus changed the world. He didn't start with masses; He chose only twelve people, teaching them to pray, not preach. His

181

Communion table was simple but symbolic of Himself, only two things, bread and wine, representing His complete Gospel, forgiveness of sin and healing for the body. His message was similar, a two-point sermon, "Love God and people," plain and easy-to-follow instructions. We have complicated the directions.

Women are "blue" because they are breathing improperly. John 20:22 says that after Jesus' resurrection He breathed His Spirit upon His disciples and that Spirit lives within us. If I had the spirit of Shakespeare, I could write poetry like his. If I had the spirit of Mozart, I would compose his music. Had I the spirit of Carl Lewis, I could have run and jumped in the Olympics as he did. If I had the spirit of Raphael, I could paint as he did.

We have a greater Spirit than theirs. John 14:12 says, "Greater things than I have done, you shall do with My Spirit in you, for I go to My Father to ask Him to send you the Source of creativity and power" (author's paraphrase). Let Him breathe into your spirit.

There is rest and energy in activity when you are yoked with, linked with, Jesus the Resurrection. It is not how much strength *we have,* but how much strength we allow Him *to pour into us!* "Ye shall receive *power,* after that the Holy Ghost is come upon you" (Acts 1:8).

You have energy because you need it. God will not give you energy to sit and eat and watch "soaps," but He will if you are investing in people and making yourself valuable to Him. He always insures His investments and takes care of His equipment and valuable tools.

My friend Barbara became so stressed she had headaches for a year. She was so busy she didn't have time for husband or family. In general her life was going downhill fast even though her work was "for God." One day as she ran into the bathroom to brush her teeth before an appointment, a voice spoke in her inner chamber. She was struck with the truth of the words. She needed to get back to the basics. "You are either doing more than I told you to do, or you are not taking My strength to do it with."

Appropriating His strength calls for faith and obedience. The Old Testament relates a story of Elijah who was miraculously fed by ravens. But for this to happen, Elijah had to obey God's word and travel eastward to a certain brook. First Kings 17:4 says, "I have commanded the ravens to feed thee *there*." Now the supply of strength we need will arrive where God has ordered it to be shipped. If we are where God wants us to be, He supplies His strength. Find His "there" for you. Tune in to His guidance, His direction.

In Canada I met the Rev. Ev, a black woman minister. She told me how she used to fret and strain in preparation to speak, always trying to squeeze out the anointing of the Spirit before stepping up to the microphone. But the Lord finally calmed her by saying, "I'll meet you at the mike."

Resting in the Lord and appropriating His strength is hard for some people to grasp. It's like the lesson my grandmother, Mom Perky, once taught me. Right before I moved to North Dakota she called me up. "Betty, you're moving away and I'm eighty-three and not well. I may never see you again, so I want you to come spend a day with me. I'll bake you an apple pie, and we'll talk and pray together."

I dropped everything (the packed boxes were stacked to the ceiling) and went.

When I arrived, she wiped her floury hands on the front of her yellow paisley cobbler apron, then grabbed and hugged me close. When she had the bottom crust in the pan, she piled up the apples, sprinkled on cinnamon, brown sugar, and white sugar.

Then she hunted for a second and gasped, "Oh, no, I can't find my nutmeg." Immediately she turned the statement into a prayer, "O Lord, will You find my nutmeg?"

I immediately thought the worst, *She's losing her marbles, getting senile.* And I said, "Mom Perky, I'll answer that prayer for you, I'm taller than you are." I searched high and low but couldn't come up with the goods. In the meantime, she rolled out the top crust. As she sculpted a palm tree in the center, someone knocked on the back door. Being the one with clean hands, I opened the door to find a squatty young woman holding a box of, you guessed it, *nutmeg,* in her right hand. I thought I had seen a ghost. I could not talk, just took the box from her hand. She explained, "I borrowed your grandma's nutmeg about six weeks ago and forgot to return it. Just two minutes ago, like a bolt of lightning out of the sky, something reminded me to bring it back."

"See, I'm not crazy," Mom Perky remarked. "I talk to Him about everything while I'm here alone. Betty, your problem is you're too smart to understand. You sing the old song 'What a friend we have in Jesus . . . oh, what peace we often forfeit, oh, what needless pain we bear, all because we do not carry everything to God in prayer!' Not just big things but *everything.*"

My grandmother's simple world was grounded in her simple trust in her friend Jesus.

Do you remember the story of Mary and Martha, sisters who opened their home to Jesus? The Gospel says that Mary sat at the Lord's feet listening to what He said. But Martha was distracted by all the preparations that had to be made. Martha interrupted their conversation and said, "Lord, tell her to help me." But what did Jesus answer? "Martha, Martha . . . you are worried and upset about many things, but only one thing is needed. Mary has chosen what is better, and it will not be taken away from her" (Luke 10:41, NIV).

What is the one thing that is needed? A simple relationship with Jesus. That is grounded in His words to us—as found in the Word. Putting God on hold until you attain your hold is like a fly clinging to a bullet.

Satan has been confusing people and families, complicating their sense of reasoning ever since he approached Eve in the Garden. If he can't get you to sin, he will overload you with responsibility and confuse you.

We get much too busy working for God to love and worship God, too busy working for our husband and children to love them or look at their eyes, touch them, see them, sit at the foot of their beds, or near them on the floor.

Worry, fear, and anxiety are playmates; they are little demonic authors of confusion. Worry is a cycle of inefficient thought whirling about a center of fear. It is a woman's worst enemy. Don't spend today's grace on tomorrow's problems.

Although it's our spiritual lives that need to be simplified, it's often our physical possessions that can distract us and cause us to . be "worried and upset about many things." Martha, the perfect hostess, was concerned that the food and table be properly prepared. Can there be anything wrong with that? Well, yes, if it causes us to worry and fret and rely on our own strength, if we're doing it because we're so concerned about what others think of us.

You would be surprised how much you can do *without*. Start cleaning out your attic, garage, or closets. I had a sale and got $328 for "didn't needs." (Eventually, we will leave it all behind anyway. See 1 Timothy 6:7.)

Organize or agonize. Each morning I make a list of things that must be done that day. I then number them, according to priority. If the insignificant are omitted, no big loss. Most of us don't have too much to do, but our duties are improperly distributed.

Our greatest enemy is discontent. "Godliness + contentment = *great gain!*" (1 Timothy 6:6). She is rich who is satisfied!

Look at people you know well. No one has everything. The women who are wealthy are sometimes frail. Sometimes the intelligent are alone; the perfect figure may have an "air head"; another woman may be jolly but poor.

Remember, this is not heaven. There may come a time when you are called to push ahead to another life structure, but always move with caution. Some women think if they could just have another baby, have a different mate, be more spiritual, or do more charitable acts, they'd be happy—or worthy. Singles want marriage. Mothers with small kids feel trapped, want freedom. If our hair is straight, we curl. If we are fair, we want a suntan. Some press harder on the accelerator, play more tennis, run more laps, give bigger parties, donate more money to God, find younger flesh to take to bed. Some women use their careers or families and children as a substitute for solving their personal problems. They pack life with activity to avoid decisions. Many women have only three securities: men, money, and church activity. If you're running down like an old clock, wind up, plug into the source, Jesus.

Remember, wherever you are Jesus is there! Stress will come after you; peace doesn't. You must go after it. As Psalm 34:14 says, "Seek peace, and pursue it." If a submarine submerges so deep that the outside pressure becomes greater than the cabin pressure, it will collapse. That doesn't need to happen to us because He who is in us is greater than he who is in the world (see

1 John 4:4). We simply must appropriate His strength by spending time with Him. Daily devotions are vital. Fifteen minutes may be enough, but, if it's possible, forget time and catch a sense of eternity!

Why is it so important to stay in tune with God and to not encumber ourselves with the things of this world? Because the Scriptures say that we are always to be ready for the return of our Lord. If we are listening and in tune with God's pitch we will be in harmony with the trumpet—the "last trump" that shall sound at the end of this dispensation and the beginning of forever.

We will rise again just as He was resurrected, if we have called on His name (see Romans 10:13). Jesus will split the eastern sky and we will rise whether we walk the earth or are buried. First Corinthians 15:52 says, "In a moment, in the *twinkling of an eye* [that's swift] . . . the trumpet shall sound, and the dead shall be raised incorruptible, and *we* shall be changed"!

When talking about the last days Jesus said, "Be careful, or your hearts will be weighed down with dissipation, drunkenness and the anxieties of life, and that day will close on you unexpectedly like a trap" (Luke 21:34, NIV).

Earlier in Luke when Jesus again talks about the last days He refers to an Old Testament woman who held her earthly possessions too tightly. Luke 17:32 is a short verse: "Remember Lot's wife!" Then Jesus goes on to say, "Whoever tries to keep his life will lose it, and whoever loses his life will preserve it"(NIV).

Do you remember the story of Lot's wife? When angels warned that she should leave Sodom she ran from the city, but when fire fell on the home she was fleeing, she turned around for one last yearning glance that proved disastrous. The Genesis account says she was turned into a pillar of salt.

Last August I was in Indianola, Iowa, during the great air

balloon race. The atmosphere of the city tingled. Red, orange, yellow, and green balloons were painted on walls of restaurants. Air balloons were printed on the napkins and brochures and streamers hung on every street! As I watched the takeoff on the evening news my heart quickened because I realized that we are going to experience an even greater event, and greater airlift when Jesus comes again to take us out of this world before it is destroyed by fire. I don't argue whether a mad scientist will trigger a nuclear holocaust or an angel will call fire down from heaven. I'm just staying in tune so I hear that trumpet call.

Some of today's prophetic teachers will probably be so busy debating post-tribulation, mid-tribulation, and pre-tribulation that they won't realize that Jesus has come—and they missed it.

Jesus said, "In such an hour as ye think not the Son of man cometh" (Matthew 24:44; Luke 12:40).

Our call to be in tune is *simply*, "Be ye also ready." For it will happen suddenly (Mathew 24:44).

APPENDIX

UNSAVED CHILDREN
Vicky Hagen #21
1804 S. Lincoln
Aberdeen, S.D. 57401

SUICIDE
Ruth Hammond
1027 Green Haven Dr.
W. Columbia, S.C. 29169

BACK TROUBLE
Clyde Strickland
730 N. 264 E. Ave.
Catoosa, Ok. 74015

WIDOWS
Katherine Fulton
269 Bleecker St.
New York, N.Y. 10014

SINGLE PARENT
Carolyn Bellar
4404 Mellowood Cir.
Knoxville, Tenn. 37920

HEALING
Dwight Fearing
117 Orchard
Sisseton, S.D. 57262

SINGLE WANTS MATE
Jean O'Connell
123 Westview Terrace
Berlin, Ct. 06037

ALCOHOLIC DELIVERANCE
Marge Block
4-301, 17481 W. 16th
Golden, Colo. 80401

WEIGHT
Pat Salisbury
R.2 Box 165-E
Lindale, Tx. 75771

DIVORCE
Ron & Vena Poole
162 Church St.
Sault Ste. Marie
Ontario, Can. P6A6M6

SMOKING—DRUGS
Larry Young
Box 5712
Phoenix, Az. 85010

DEPRESSION
Clare Payne
1618 Clarendon
Longview, Tx. 75601

LESBIAN SET FREE
Candace Grason
3156 Quartz Lane #1
Fullerton, Cal. 92631-2550

DEATH OF A CHILD
Patty Carpenter
Box 387 109 N.3rd
Newman Grove, Neb. 68758

189

PREMATURE SICK BABIES
Patty Flugstad
605 Hillcrest
Webster City, Ia. 50595

STROKE
Rosa Willis
P.O. 151
Lloyd, Fla. 32337

PREGNANCY—BABY
Joyce Moon
P.O. 13757
St. Petersburg, Fla. 33733-3757

HELP FOR HURTING PARENT
Focus on the Family
P.O. Box 500
Arcadia, Ca. 91006

CANCER
Rose Osha
Box 304
Washington, Ind. 47501

CANCER
Carol Sullivan
R.21 Box 556
Terre Haute, Ind. 47802

LISTENING POST
Paul Priddy
P.O. 4314
Pasadena, Tx. 77502

M.S.
Eleanor Olson
Leonard, N.D. 58052 (summer)
456 S. Nassau (winter)
Mesa, Az. 85206

PRAYS FOR BLIND
Betty Davis
418 Essex Dr.
Tallahassee, Fla. 32304

AUTISTIC-RETARDED CHILD
Jackie Ransdell
3333 Ocotea Street
Raleigh, N.C. 27607

UNSAVED HUSBAND
Shirley Wyatt
Crestwood Farm
R.2 Box 30
Rantoul, Ill. 61866

EPILEPSY
Patty Opsal
4007 Elm, Apt. 105
Rapid City, S.D. 57701

SUPPORT GROUP FOR FAMILIES OF HOMOSEXUALS
Barbara Johnson
Spatula Ministry Box 444
La Habra, Ca. 90631

MENOPAUSE AND P.M.S.
Ruth Denny
990 Dawn Lane
Terre Haute, Ind. 47802

ARTHRITIS
Florence Jensen
1533-13th Av. N.
Ft. Dodge, Ia. 50501

*HYPER, NERVOUS
CHILDREN*
Sandra Parker
1210 Annette
Longview, Tx. 75604

PASTORS' WIVES
Carolyn Nelson
1409 Pebble Beach Rd.
Mitchell, S.D. 57301

FINANCES
Kathy Smith
120 Urbana Way
Athens, Ga. 30606

HEART TROUBLE
Esther Zink
Ellendale, N.D. 58436